THE OUTBACK MUSICIAN

BY PHIL CIRCLE

One Guy's Story of

Surviving 30 Years as an Independent Musician

In the Modern American Music Industry.

Although every precaution has been taken to verify the accuracy of the information contained herein, the author and publisher assume no responsibility for any errors or omissions. No liability is assumed for damages that may result from the use of information contained within.

Copyright © 2017 by Phil Circle
All rights reserved.

No part of this book may be reproduced in any written, electronic, recording, or photocopying without written permission of the publisher or author. The exception would be in the case of brief quotations embodied in critical articles or reviews. For information, contact Phil Circle at philcirclemusic@gmail.com.

Published by Phil Circle and Guilt By Association, Chicago

Books may be purchased by sending $15US to the author:
Phil Circle, 1902 W. Morse Ave. #3, Chicago, IL, 60626 USA;
1-773-936-4953; PayPal with philcirclemusic@gmail.com; or
on his website www.philcirclemusic.com/pay_here
Mention the book and your address in the info field.
Physical copies and PDF versions are available.

Publisher: Phil Circle and Guilt By Association
Editorial Input: Megan Corse
Cover Design: Pedro Bopp
Cover Photos: Charlie Higher of Higher Photography

Thank you to Ben Ortiz for a final read-through before publication, and for your valuable input.

Thanks to Beth, Dave, Di, Ed, Frank, Greg, Jeremiah, John, Katie, Kyle, and Maya for your support in getting this book to the public. You are true patrons of the arts.

Second Edition
Printed in the United States of America

What's Happening?

Let me introduce myself for the obvious reasons. I'm Phil Circle. I'm nobody any more than anybody else. I've been through as many, less than or more hardships than anyone. I have achieved equality, inferiority, and superiority with regard to any other person's success. How do we weigh success? For my part, it comes to doing what one loves.

I love to write stuff down. I love to tell stories. I'm a writer and a musician, so logically, I also write songs. I do a few other things. That's what I do to be happy: I write and play music and do other stuff. Sometimes I write a song. Sometimes I write an article or blog. Sometimes, I never get it past my thoughts and feelings to the page and they bounce about my cluttered mind. They become a part of the orally transmitted tidbits I love to share. That's the other thing. I love to share. So, there you have it. Happiness in a nutshell for Phil Circle amounts to sharing. After years of people bothering me to write down my stories and anecdotes, here it is. This will be my second go of it. The first one was about as non-linear as an acid trip. This effort has become more along a thread, more of an overall story.

This Irish Gypsy adopted son of a Welsh raconteur has made a point of adding color. You may rest and read assured that this is not fiction, however. I don't add a shiny coat of paint to any of the darker or more brutal discussions. I'm not here to coddle. I don't avoid the rough details of myself, or my views. I'm not here to lie. I don't see a horrible business environment for the independent artist, either. There is always room for change. There is always room for hope. What was that line? Revolutions are built on hope. Here's hoping!

I'm here to share my experience, maybe add a little hope, and to leave some information and lessons to ponder. I want you to know that my 30+ years involved in this industry has been worth every second. My fifty-one years and counting on this planet are a delight, in spite. I am happily counting on more.

Now, I'm off to ramble, to hear the sound of my writer's voice lengthening on the page, and bring you on a delightful, frightful, high-five-filled journey through creative thought and the distractions it brings. Sometimes, it's romantic. Sometimes it's drudgery. Sometimes it's downright dark and painful, at least to watch. Sometimes it's absolute magic and miracles.

My voice takes on the various settings of the stories and reflections. Some stories are written in the third person, some use more of my vernacular. Others are in the first person and may take on an air of instruction. This was all by design at the time they were written. Many were imported and assimilated from older writings into this book. The spoken or creative voice will speak with ease or tension depending on the setting and message.

I'll get down in the mud with this. I won't say I'm not arrogant. I'm capable of it. I've been guilty of it. I won't deny my own fear of people, my social anxiety, stage fright, or writer's block. I won't avoid or deny my need for approval, my unending fight against laziness, my manic-depressive nature, my hard fought battles with addiction, my disgust and admiration for mainstream success, or my desire for more of what I already have. It's called being human. Or, to quote a Russian artist I hung out with for a time, it sounds like life to me. I hope that every creative soul will know they are never alone. I hope that all who observe us, as if through the cage at a zoo, will come to realize they are one of us. We are, without question in this mind, all a creative entity.

Whether you're in the room fully immersed in the discussion or watching through the window with curiosity, I trust this will be a quick enough read. I entrust myself to your patience while I continue to do what I've dedicated my life to so far: understanding the human condition through the arts. I've made this a book of mostly short excerpts. This should help in the easy-scan read while sitting at a café or bar, or on the toilet.

While I've been a communicator in one form or another for most of my life, it took me some time to realize this could be the answer when someone asks, "What do you do?" I'm pretty comfortable with the title now. For business purposes, it's usually singer-songwriter-guitarist.

Having fallen in love with communication, I now take much of what I've read, pondered, spun about in my head, and just plain randomly sprouted and make it public. Thank you kindly for reading.

Hold your head up. Peace.

-Phil

Every person that has contributed to this book in whatever way has joined a movement away from the mainstream and commercial arts. This stands true of every person who buys this book, as well. The money made from sales of this book doesn't go into the pocket of Phil Circle for food and rent and such. It is all flipped back into itself to print more copies of the book and to fund other creative projects. For a songwriter, there are always new recordings ready to be made. For a producer, there's always a new show idea that requires testing in front of a live audience. For the front man of a full band and an advocate of the arts, each member of the band gets paid for rehearsals and live shows, regardless of the income from the particular show. This is even true when services are offered for a fundraising event. For a DIY advocate and someone dedicated to empowering independent artists, there are constant little business experiments to show what works, and what doesn't. All of this work funds itself through the sale of merchandise, including this book. Thank you for joining or furthering the movement away from the mainstream.

On The Craft

Thoughts, Experiences, and Streaming Ramblings Related to Being a Creative Type

Stage Fright And Other Less Scary Things

The first time I played one of my songs for a couple friends, I was so desperately nervous that I turned my back and closed my eyes while performing. I lifted my lids with trepidation after finishing the tune. My friends had moved around to stand in front of me. Their mouths were hanging open, eyes wide. I wasn't sure whether they were impressed or disgusted. Then one of them said,

"That was amazing."

I breathed, smiled shyly, and whispered "thanks." I felt a notch in my belt. I had read somewhere that to focus on fear or failure was a waste of energy, that one should count only the victories. I typically try to do this. I know I haven't always succeeded, but I've certainly given it a solid try.

I can't remember how the song went or what it was even called. I think it was in the key of A minor. I've probably used ideas from it in songs I've written since then. I was twenty years old. It was after this experience that I began performing publicly. At first I hit open mic nights or took my guitar to parties. I was determined to gain confidence and lose the stage fright. I found my confidence through working in front of people. I still get stage fright. I was also determined to be heard. This, I accomplished. Extensively. Soon I was playing longer sets of my music here and there.

In dealing with stage fright over the years, I've learned to remind myself that there's a good reason for it: I care. I want to put on a great show for people, to entertain them. Gradually, another thing dawned on me: It's all about the audience. I'm giving them all I've got and I want them to be happy, to get that therapy that music provides. So, I always try to remind myself before getting on stage that it's not about *me*. It's about *them*. Give the crowd all you can stand. It works. It's tricky. It's not a cure all. But it starts the work.

My first official "gig" was playing music for a play a co-worker of mine at a sandwich shop (one of my three jobs) had written. I put together a bunch of instrumental guitar work, some stuff by other artists and some ideas I either threw out or recycled later. It was just to be background, sort of incidental music. I was not yet quite clear on the concepts regarding fear that I've just shared. I was so fucking nervous that when the director asked me where would be a good place to play from I pointed to the back of the theater. Up at the back of the theater, behind the seats, there was a little wall with an aisle on the backside of it.

"Do you need amplification?"

"No," I said, "it'll fill the room."

(Apparently I played that giant guitar mariachis use?)

So throughout opening night of the play, I sat there peering over this small wall in a dark space in the far back of a half-filled theater playing the music I'd arranged and diligently practiced. At the end of the show, when bows were taken, the director pointed up towards me to thank me. I stood up with my guitar, smiling like an idiot. The entire crowd turned with a look on their faces like "there was music?" The next night I was down in front of the stage.

In 1988, I worked nine months without a day off, on three to four hours sleep a night. I was determined to sock away enough money to quit my jobs (all three of them) and work in music full time. Instead, I became so ill that I was hospitalized. I opted to move to Albuquerque, New Mexico, to enjoy a better climate for my health and a slower pace of life than Chicago. I arrived there March 28, 1989, and stayed for nearly three years. This is where I first truly cut my teeth on live shows.

There was an open mic at EJ's Coffee Shop near my place. My apartment amounted to a converted garage. It was easy to want to get out, and I would frequent the many nights of live music at the coffee shop. Playing the open stage repeatedly led me to some actual shows of my own.

Suffering from fainting-level stage fright still, I took the advice of a mentor of mine in Buddhism... play from your Buddha Nature... your enlightened nature. I wasn't sure I had such a thing, but wrote it on all my little hand-written set lists.

I felt like I was going to keel over every time I got up to play, so I'd close my eyes and pretend I was alone at home. I got vertigo from the darkness. Still, I would persist. Anything was better than seeing the people staring up at me scrutinizing my every mistake and wondering at my shaking hands and sweaty brow. At least losing that distraction to a degree might allow me to throw myself into it. Then I'd open my eyes, see the crowd, and want to keel over again.

Somehow, I survived many nights on the edge of this precipice. Somehow, I booked more shows at various venues in Albuquerque. Somehow, I survived those gigs and many more since. As I said, I still get nerves. One thing that has yet to happen: I haven't fainted or otherwise lost consciousness at a gig. Well, unless not remembering anything the next day counts.

Then there's the question of undue or overwhelming anxiety. Here's what I've come to understand there: It's all ego. Yep. That's it. You see ego is not just something that causes arrogance. It's also the culprit where crippling anxiety is concerned, or low self-esteem, or being over helpful. I'm not so important that a mistake in my performance is going to have such a negative effect on the world that it warrants heart attack inducing fear. Nobody cares *that* much about my skill level at any given show. It's unlikely they're listening that carefully. If they are, it's because I grabbed their attention in some way. That'd be a good thing! Nobody is looking for or hearing the solvent to the world's problems in my songs. Maybe they hear hope, maybe they hear fear, maybe they hear resilience, opinions, anger, love, or any number of things. Once again, if they hear it, I've conveyed it. They were most likely listening for something, too. A technical mistake won't loosen their grip on the message. I'm not that fucking important. I have *some* confidence in who I am, but am not overwhelmed with self importance. It's a tricky balance, but well worth keeping. Did I mention, I'm not that fucking important?

Creative Anxiety And The Chicken And The Egg

I lie on my 30 year-old wife's shoulder. She's brilliant, beautiful, and successful. I'll be 48 six weeks from when I write this. I say,

"I hope I can eventually do something in life. You know what I mean? I know I've done something, but…"

She runs her hand across my head and kisses me.

"Yes."

She gets it. She knows I hate the economic aspect. She knows I want to simply create. She knows that I revolve around the need to communicate. She sees and feels everything I do. She also sees how I've influenced people, how many other artists have turned to me, and the way that I give my all to help them.

Still…

Why do I have to worry about the simple shit in life? When did my job become that of a promoter, a booker, a manager, a producer, an accountant… when all I intended was

11

to share this odd view of the world through these creative goggles?

"Do you still love me?"

"Of course I do."

I suddenly jump from the couch, run to the kitchen, pour myself a shot, and scamper to my room to write it all down.

Now, if only for an instant, I feel who I am, what I am. I feel my purpose, as ridiculous as it sounds, with all the pretension it implies. Now I am being Phil Circle.

Which came first, the urge or the reaction? Were the questions a series of complaints or a simple debriefing to clear the mind? Or, were they exactly the expression that needed a page to lean on?

We all know from our first remembrances who we intend to be, if we trust our recall. As children, we have these dreams asleep and awake. Then we grow old and jaded and let them go. There's this need to be the person we are expected to be. Get married, have children, buy a house, get a "respectable" job, contribute to the community.

I ask this:

Can we live without the arts?

I'll ask again and with more vinegar.

Can we survive without what people of the arts give us every fucking day to make our existences more tolerable?

I know that I never could.

My insanity alone required outside expression until I came by it myself. My curiosity just fueled my desire.

I know that this may be what drove me this direction.

I know that while I love what I do, I have a tendency to fight life as any human does. What I enjoy that few others apparently do is the immediate satisfaction of doing what I'm doing now:

Write it down… privately, on your own terms. Nobody needs to see it.

I highly encourage this exercise. I do it a lot.

Speak it, in your own voice, in your immediate mood, with all the passion you have. You will feel closer to your Spirit than you ever have. You may even bring someone else to this place should you choose to share. You'll find it whisping out into your words to people. And look! You're now contributing to your community. How about that shit? The need to express *is* a respectable and much needed enterprise.

Class is over for now. No one will be graded. Do your work in your own time on your own terms. You have a lifetime to finish the experiment.

Practicing As An Obsessive Pastime

I never thought I was good at getting enough practice time in, but I look back and I think I'm not good at it now. Maybe it's hubris, but I require less to keep my chops after nearly 40 years of playing. When I do get in extra time, of course I feel more fluid in my performances. I also get to enjoy new levels of playing and discover new creative ideas. Go figure. It still works.

Thinking about the days when I started gigging, I believe I was a bit obsessive. Before leaving Chicago for Albuquerque, I was barely sleeping. Even after I'd get home from one or two of my three jobs, I'd leave my girlfriend in the other room. Then, I'd go into this giant walk-in closet I had set up for practicing and recording, and play until 2 or 3am. I don't remember where she put her clothes. On Sundays, my boss at my primary job would let me bring my guitar to the gas station and practice when it was slow as long as things were stocked and clean, and I would make my girlfriend drive anytime we went somewhere, so I could sit in the backseat and practice.

In New Mexico, I was just as constant. When I was working a consistent job--I started doing odd jobs when I first arrived--I got home at about 4pm most days. I wouldn't allow myself to watch T.V. or eat until 10pm. I would dedicate all of my time to various music-related work, especially practicing little runs on my guitar and working out my vocal exercises. Once, a neighbor came over and told me to "stop yelling," so I put some Native blankets on the wall that we shared. At 10pm I'd turn on the T.V. and eat, usually something like Ramen or rice and beans, as I was pretty poor. However, my guitar would sit on its stand next to the couch, and every time a commercial came on, I'd play some more. Doing that amounts to about twenty more minutes of practice per hour of television. Yes, I did the math. I also figured out how many hours are in a week and pester my students about it to this day. There are 168.

I had a student in Chicago some years ago. He happened to be attending Columbia College where I graduated in 1997. At his first voice lesson, he told me he had "massive ADHD." I explained that music would get around that tricky trigger. Musical performance uses the entire brain. We commenced.

Each week, he'd come in with an impressive list of questions and observations. When practicing came up he explained that in order to not annoy his neighbors late at night, he'd go up to the roof of his building, 35 stories high, and practice his vocal work there. It was winter at the time, and his building was on Lake Michigan. Talk about dedication! And what ADHD was he referring to?

Treating music as the language that it is, working at it for the love of it, and simply approaching it as a given part of one's daily routine, it's really pretty easy to create consistent practice habits. As with anything else, some days may be crammed with a lot, and time spent may be diminished. Once it's ingrained, it's a rare day that music isn't just like breathing or eating or taking a dump. When you don't, you get sick or cranky. Keep your mood up, as well as the mood of those around you. Practice and play every day. Be regular and healthy.

Creative Discipline And Other Oxymorons

I once was reading a book, <u>Becoming A Writer</u> by Dorothea Brande, written in 1934. In it, there was an exercise for bringing out your creative voice, your writer's voice. That's the unique style that we all ultimately possess when we write, much like our manner of speech. It's what brings alive some writings, and it's the lack of it that makes others dull. Every great storyteller has a voice that is specific to their style.

The exercise involved writing twice a day for 30 days; once when you wake up in the morning, again at some time you choose later in the day. Each time, you have to write without censorship whatever comes to mind without stopping for at least ten minutes... in pen. Don't think twice about what you're about to write or go back and read it over to follow a thought. Write whatever comes to mind and heart. Don't know what to write? Write about that!

Again, do this for 30 days without going back to read any of it. If you miss even one session, you have to start over. If you can't go for 30 days, you don't have the discipline it takes to be a writer or artist of any kind. Developing the skills necessary to create well, one needs discipline. I know, it goes counter to our feeling that we should wait for inspiration. I can't tell you how many songs or writings started with me expressing that I had nothing inspiring me… just saying.

After 30 days, put the notebook on a shelf or in a drawer for a week. Then, some day when you have plenty of time, grab the book, pour a beverage, and read it cover to cover. You'll be surprised what you discover. When I did this, I put three entries together into a song, for instance.

Now, you may think you've got the idea ten days into it and can stop. I had a highly talented student who showed great potential, and he did that. He's not doing music anymore... didn't have the discipline driven by the desire. Making the decision based on desire still requires real action and follow-through. Another student of mine did it for forty days, and I had to tell her to at least grab what she'd done and take time to read it. She was extremely driven. I coached her on three instruments and songwriting. Last I spoke to her, she was on her way to tour China solo after leaving a very well known band.

Working artists are not lazy. They can't afford to be. You have to let the fire blaze, and this means you're constantly thinking of more that you could be doing. You're always adding fuel. As a singer/songwriter/guitarist, I have five basic skills that need to constantly be honed: my voice, my guitar playing, my writing, my ability to create melody, and my creative voice.

Creativity And The Entrepreneur Collide

Is there anything more self-indulgent than being an artist? Do we do it for the right reasons? Does it matter?

We give this gift and feel bad when folks open it and say, "oh, um, gee, uh, thanks"; and feel great when they say

17

with joy, "this was just what I needed!" even if we thought it was simple to give.

While we may not do it for financial gain, we need some; while we say it's all for the fun, we work very hard for it; while we say we don't give a shit what people think, it's often foremost in our minds. We need approval, we need the various gains... just as all people do with anything. Thank an artist. Buy their work, if only a download or CD. Listen to it, identify with it, and share its beauty with others. Attach yourself to it as you would anything or anybody. Music is a part of all of us.

Remember, you need it too. Life would be empty without the arts. Now turn off mainstream radio. Turn on and open your mind to what may be just across the street.

As an artist, make your work widely available. People want it. People need it. Regardless of what you hear on mainstream radio, listeners want something different. Give it to them. Why? Oh, I don't know, but…

Is there anyone more self-indulgent than the American consumer?

Songwriting And Rigorous Honesty

I was reading my third book by Henry. I knocked out Tropic of Cancer and Tropic of Capricorn a long time ago. I haven't yet finished Sexus.

In it, he writes at one point, "Every day we slaughter our finest impulses." How true! By not letting ourselves write with the utmost honesty, as Henry Miller most certainly did, we risk losing much of the power of our work, not to mention our creative voice.

While attending Columbia College Chicago for my music degree I also worked through a good part of their fiction writing curriculum. I noticed I wasn't getting many A's. This annoyed my sensibilities as the son of a writer who had also taught English. I was pretty certain I had a good handle on the language. Rather than let it screw with my GPA, I went to the guy who eventually became one of my advisors toward graduation. I asked him (with much posturing, no doubt) what the deal was. He very patiently pointed out the problem.

"Phil, you do have a great grasp on the language, but there's more to it than that. When I'm reading your stuff you begin to make these great unique little threads of description that draw the reader in… and then you tug it away. You go back to playing it safe and rest on proper grammar and punctuation."

I was depriving the reader of my writer's voice. Or worse, I was giving a little tease of it then pulling the rug out just as they were getting hooked. My professor (Eric May is his name) set me up with a private tutor to work some exercises specific to developing this. I received nothing but A's from there forward. I had to learn to be frightfully honest with my style of story telling. I had to be uncomfortable sometimes with my own quirkiness.

We might also make other people uncomfortable in our non-censorship with our feelings or quirks, but so be it. We can't afford to be plain good with the language or we risk becoming generic. If we don't let our deepest impulses drive our art, what does it become? I'll quote my good friend and musical collaborator Lem: increasing waves of blandness. Let some spice clear the sinuses once in awhile. Give it your unique flavor.

There was a DJ for an online radio show in Chicago who played a lot of my material. One song he featured regularly was called "The Life of Any Man." It describes the feelings of being alone and standing on a razor's edge, when a simple revelation causes you to throw yourself a rope. You realize you are living a life that could be that of any man, any human. You are never truly alone.

This DJ called me up one afternoon and related this story:

"Phil, you know all the tough times I've been going through lately. Well, yesterday, it came to a head. I was walking across the Ashland Avenue Bridge (by Clybourn Ave. where it crosses the Chicago River). I was horribly depressed. I stopped and looked at the river, wanting to jump in. Then, your song "The Life of Any Man" popped into my head and I realized I wasn't alone in the world after all. I just wanted to thank you for saving my life, man."

Ponder this the next time you think you're being "too honest" in your music.

More Notes On Songwriting

I'm not a huge fan of songwriting classes but have coached people in the songwriting process.

Wait, what? Phil, you ask, did you just say you are not a fan of songwriting classes? Why yes, I did. Stay with me here. As I use the standard 20/20 hindsight to scan more than two decades of doing this, I find that teaching and coaching have become two slightly different things. And yet, they remain related and attached to one another. The coach forces you to learn through action and points you in the direction of the end zone with a strategy in mind, but only after the teacher has given you the list of skills and knowledge required to run the plays. Put these aspects together and you have a delicate balance. You also have the beginnings of how to go about songwriting. I'm not big on formulas, but I'll give it a shot.

One problem with learning songwriting is that most likely the only theory that really helps is music theory. That's a separate class. It also needs to be related and applied to your instrument of choice and requires a lot of outside work. Take it, I highly recommend it; it will be helpful in communicating with the musicians you hire to record and perform live. It will also give you a great knowledge of all the possibilities open to you. Are you worried about theory throwing off your creative impulses? Don't be. Lem, that guy I just mentioned? His music theory is immaculate, and he's one of the most fearlessly creative people I know.

It's true that we need to develop the ability to step back, to look and listen objectively. This can go a long way after you've written a song and help a great deal with the production process. The actual writing of a song is something one dives into with pure subjectivity, however.

So, let's talk about this process and make the assumption that I know something about it. Regardless of the number of songs I've written and all the friendly press I've received, everyone's sense of "good music" is different. Take what I write here as fuel for your fire or with a grain of salt. See if it makes sense to you, let it germinate, take some action based on what inspires you—then adjust your seatbelt and try a different route just to test it out. One thing I assure you of is this: you will very likely continue to reinvent yourself as a songwriter. The minute you think you've got a really solid handle on songwriting, you're probably full of shit and your days as an evolving artist may be over.

The creative process is ongoing, and yet where does it all begin? How do you know you have what it takes to write a song? Try and finish one. Let me rephrase that. Just finish the damned thing! All artists work from a sense of what actors typically call "the human condition." If you're a living, breathing human, you develop your own views of how the world works and respond to it. You then express this to people through everything you say and do. Now toss a few chords together with your guitar or keyboard and start writing. Throw some random lyrics at it. Sing about the wall you're staring at. Who cares? Start saying something. Think and feel out loud. Try not to think of a musical genre; just allow your own worldview to speak. Then, as I said, finish it. Leave judgment for later. One fellow songwriter friend of mine put it nicely when he said, "write a song and throw it out." If you question yourself throughout the process, you'll never get it done. Just speak your heart, write it down, play it to death, add whatever occurs to you, play it to death. Then set it aside and forget about it. Give it maybe a week or so, then go back and run through your new tune. Play it to death. Now decide if you have anything more to add. Remember, you may find that getting it in front of an unsuspecting audience at an open mic is a good way to go.

You may have noticed I've skipped (until now!) the question of the structural approach. There isn't a formula, only an endless number of possibilities for the start to finish. Everyone will give you a different approach because everyone has a different approach. You want the verse, chorus, verse, chorus, bridge pivoting off the relative minor approach? Fine, if it works. Bob Dylan doesn't seem to have enjoyed that approach, and all it got him was a Nobel Prize. Basically, try everything until something works. You are under absolutely no obligation to anyone to write a specific kind of song in a specific kind of way. It is and always will be entirely up to you. Do you like to lay down some musical ideas first or start with lyrics? Do you have several scraps of paper with various notions scrawled on them from which you construct a final song? Maybe it's some combination of all of the above. I've found that every time I complete a series of recordings for a release, my approach to songwriting will change somehow. Every album completes another story in my life. I've matured and/or evolved, and so will my approach. What worked for me ten years ago doesn't necessarily work today and vice versa. Allow yourself to discover the possibilities, complete each song in your own time and on your own terms. Finally, be willing to toss out or recycle ideas you look back over that don't give you the feeling that you've completely expressed what you set out to say. Tell your story and stick to it. Your expression and your sense of the human condition is what others will gravitate to when it's given from the heart.

So, to review, I've created three steps at a glance:

1.   Use The Duke Ellington Rule: "If it sounds good, it IS good". Genre is irrelevant. Tell your story, and express your feelings. Leave it at that.

2.   With every fresh creation, you have re-identified yourself... know that this means your expressive style is going to most likely evolve as well.

3.   Yes, throw out your babies. You're not as brilliant as you think you are at the second that song flows forth. Set it aside for a week or two. Come back to it. Still sound and feel good? Try it in front of an audience. And please

avoid saying, "Here's a new song I wrote." Nobody cares. Just tell the story. Good response? Must be a good tune. Well done.

Why do I write songs, and will I always do so? Here's a nice example from teaching: When a new music student walks into my studio, I ask them why they want to do this.

When they say,

"I can't imagine doing anything else,"

I know I've got someone like myself and so many for whom I have great admiration... one who lives to communicate the human condition through creative expression.

The number of new songs or other creative endeavors may or may not wax or wane, but we will always have the need to create through one form or another and should never stop.

For those who aren't sure if they can write a song, I'll share what visual artist and teacher from the Bauhaus school had to say on the subject. Laszlo Moholy-Nagy said "Everyone is talented." Author Thomas Dyja put Moholy's feelings on this in a nutshell, saying *In essence, art isn't something out of reach, or strictly for display* (or recording), *it is crucial to human survival. It's a part of our biology to create.*

Even a simple song allows for subtle complexities that can really stir emotions in people. Our ears listen, our minds process, and our hearts hear. 90% of what we process happens beyond the conscious mind. We are for the most part only conscious of our response, and even then only when we're self-aware. Ultimately, our hearts respond before we think. It works the other way around, too. Our hearts feel before we think of a culturally appropriate response. Let it happen. "From the heart" is a real thing with tangible results in all that we create.

Comparisons (Just Some Thoughts)

I find that playing and singing music have a lot in common with acting.

The voice is your instrument, or one of them.

You need to use pitch and timing, and interpret rhythm.

There's a lot of memorization required.

You tell a story.

You create a character on stage, and those who do it best bring a part of themselves to that character, without fail.

You interact with an audience in some form or other.

You can work in different media.

You can write the work yourself or use something that has been written by others, then make it your own.

In some styles there is improvisation, and all styles require honest individuality in order to come across well.

It's unlikely that you have health insurance, paid vacations, or paid sick days through the job provider.

There's no minimum wage without a union.

You are immediately responsible for your own success or failure and may be an entrepreneur of sorts.

During the early years you probably lived on your friends' couches or with a significant other at times or you'd have been on the street.

You get to do something you love that the whole world needs and wants, and you may never want or need to retire.

Why We All Struggle In English Class

As I stand on the bow and I bow, I shoot my bow.

My burro that I borrowed took me to the borough where I burrowed under and went to borrow a stole that I stole.

I turned right and left, but left the right for the left because I felt right and now I write what's left.

At least the word "fuck" can be used as a verb, adverb, noun, pronoun, or adjective.

Being a Night Owl... What A Hoot

I held the dreaded day jobs back in the day. I typically showed up on time and enjoyed raises and promotions until I got to the point of no return: management. Then I'd quit. So long, and thanks for all the fish. There was one job (30 years ago!) where I had to make my way from Rogers Park in Chicago (where I live again!) to a gas and service station in suburban Skokie. I was often up until 3:30 or four in the morning and had to be at work by 8am. When I ran late, the owner would not be pleased, especially since I was his assistant manager. So, when I knew I was not going to be on time, I'd stop and grab a box of donuts. I'd arrive at work to the grimace of the owner.

"Philly, you're late."

I'd present the box of donuts.

"Eddie, I'm sorry, there was a really big line at Drunkin' Dognuts."

His eyes would light up at the prospect of gaining more weight or feeding the need for sugar that we all seemed to have, and things would be happy again. Ed was actually really good to me. I regretted leaving the job when my health failed from pushing myself way too hard through a summer of record high temperatures and drought. The doctor told me to get away from the gas fumes. He also told me I wouldn't make it past 30 due to my health problems and life style. Oops.

The thing is, while I was reliable to the day jobs I held, I was never very good in the morning. I moved from a motivation to eat, pay rent, gas up my car, and other annoying things. I also placed importance on pride in my work and tried to grab something from every job I held. I knew these jobs fed my day-to-day life with experience *and* money. Without life experience, what would I have to write about? Without money where have I to write? I actually don't think I ever hated a job I held. As for mornings, I have gotten a little better, I guess. But I still like the night.

When I was a kid, I'd often stay up all night reading books or writing stories, using a flashlight under the sheets in the event that my Mom would come check on me. She was a bit of an insomniac, it seemed. Maybe it was her combined minor (I think) mental illness and the alcohol. In the middle of the night, she'd open my door to see if I was sleeping. I'd hear her coming, turn off my flashlight, and pretend to be asleep. She'd close my door, and I'd listen for her door down the hall to shut. At that point I'd get back to my reading or writing. I recall reading a book called "Beautiful Joe" about an abused and deformed dog, about 200 pages, all in one night. I've always been this way.

As a young adult (23 or so), I read an article, in a science magazine I think, about night owls. They, whomever "they" are, had discovered that humans have different sorts of internal clocks. We aren't all ready to wake at dawn and go hunt the wooly mammoth or gather berries. As we grow older, our chemistry changes (No, shit, really?) and so does our clock. I'll attest to it speeding up!

Nowadays, I find myself waking without an alarm at hours that are sometimes just wrong. I stopped fighting it, regardless of when I get to sleep. I'll get up at 6am, and rather than roll over, grab a book to read. When I get hungry, I'll throw on the T.V. or keep reading, and eat some beans or something. Keep in mind that I can often take a nap later in the day. Yes, I said it. Nap. But I do it Jeffersonian style: 20-30 minutes, sometimes sitting up. I don't hold a silver spoon over a crystal glass to work as an alarm like Jefferson did. I have a smart phone. I feel like it cost more than his silver spoon and crystal glass.

I'll wake up again and do whatever other work I feel inclined to. If I have students that day, I'll do that. If I have a show that night, I'll prepare for that. When I'm tired again, I'll crawl into bed. It's not unusual, however, for me to hit the late evening and want to keep going. Regardless of fatigue I'll suddenly have a surge of creative energy and push myself through bleary eyes.

What I keep finding, however my own span of 24 hours works itself out, is that I often feel most creative in the dark hours. One of the interesting things about the creative mind is that it doesn't keep a schedule. Often times, I'll come jetting in the front door and as my lovely wife tries to say hello, I'll shoosh her (risking later apologies) and run to my notebook or computer to write something that's been running through my head, in order that it doesn't get jettisoned.

Here's an example. It's 3:30am. I'm on the front stoop smoking a cigarette in 10-degree weather, my ass freezing to the stair. My mind wanders through my days. The day before; the upcoming day; whatever work I have to complete; someone I've been thinking about; an experience I've just had; an experience from long ago that I've been reminded of from the threads running through my ever-overactive brain.

I begin telling a story to no one in particular. I toss my spent smoke and run back up to my music room and get to work. The next thing I know, it's dawn. It's time for some beans and a nap. Stay out from under the covers.

It is difficult, without a doubt, to allow oneself to create on these impulses. As I said previously, do it anyway. Find some way to get it down on paper, become better at memorization, or learn little tricks with cues that spurred the expression. Do whatever it takes to allow yourself to enjoy these creative moments. Coupled with discipline you develop to move the juices, these creative bursts can be very powerful and effective.

Getting Into The Stu-Stu-Studio

Everyone works differently in the studio. Some thrive in it, some struggle. The last I knew and according to a write-up about me, I had something like 130 recordings available. Damn. Where'd the time go? Oh, into my work. Sweet. It's funny how I still don't feel like I know much about the studio. Keep in mind I'm not the technical guy behind the board. I know what a volume pot is, a mute button, a microphone, and that funny little picture of peaks and valleys. I've learned some other things, though. Let me share them.

Find an engineer who likes, no, loves your music. For me, engineer and co-producer are usually one and the same for recording sessions. If this is you, make sure he or she knows how to produce and enjoys doing so. Listen to their previous works. Trust their ear. Be certain they trust yours. Be especially certain that *you* trust yours. Share your vision with absolute certainty. Let them do their work, and listen to what they say. If you're lucky, they can get inside your head and heart and help mold the audio landscape that best brings to life your stories and sentiments. Working in the studio is about collaboration. One more thing: Take your time looking for this person.

It took me a number of recording sessions to even know whether I enjoyed working in the studio. I'm so fond of the live experience, in spite of my nervousness about it, that I was unsure that I could bring my music to life in the apparently stale setting of a recording studio. I had to have the lights slightly dimmed, find just the right balance in my headphones to mimic the stage… and I found myself easily and often quickly annoyed if I couldn't find my groove.

I adjusted. By going through enough sessions over time with engineers and co-producers who could help me discover ways to create the sound I had in my head, I learned to work with this unusual approach to music. What do I mean by unusual approach? Don't forget that recording devices are a recent development in the history of music. We've found evidence of music (instruments) existing back to cave dwellers. We've been recording for just over a century. Like the idea of creating a written language for music, however, we adjusted to the idea of making something live and created in the moment into a permanent record. It still may be a little foreign to one's innate sense of things creative, though.

Getting the hang of working in the studio is like getting the hang of any other aspect of our work. Keep doing it until you find your most comfortable and effective approach. I'm quite happy in the studio now. Whenever I've written a new tune, I look forward to the possibilities for it in a studio environment as much as I look forward to getting it into solo and band settings on the live stage.

Rock Star 101

Here's a term that has taken on many meanings: "Rock Star."

We use it in so many ways these days that it can imply you are famous and rich, got the best parking spot on a crowded street, inspired someone, or even got away with something in a "cool" way. It can make implications about your arrogance or your own delusional belief in your brilliance.

I've been called "Rock Star" by people better than me, and some I perceived to be less so (an ego oops at the time). I've been called it by people who used it in admiration, and by some who used it in disgust. I've enjoyed it to help others, and I've used it to do things I'm not so proud of.

It's just a term, a colloquialism: Rock Star.

I prefer it be one of endearment, of course. I'm neither rich nor famous. There are those to whom the term has been coined because they are both rich and famous; again, some for the better, many for the worse… to theirs and others' detriment or betterment. Many of us use it in all its possible forms. I guess it's a matter of the sub-text, as to what one truly means. I'm going to be listening more carefully!

I think it'd be a better world if we could all be Rock Stars in the best possible way. Yes, this includes getting a good parking spot.

Who's Your Worst Critic? Who's Your Best?

Critic: That nasty son-of-a-bitch that has mean things to say about your work.

Critique: That helpful list of things a nice person shares with you about how to improve your work.

At least, this is what we generally hear or feel with regard to these terms.

Are you your own worst critic? You must be comparing yourself to... yourself. Bad idea. Here's what can happen.

You're having a shitty day. You listen to your song and somehow compare your work to that piece of shit you believe you are and can never escape. Nothing will ever be good enough, because you never will be. This is actually where the myth of artistic perfection comes from: total self-doubt about one's innate ability to be safe in their openness and honesty.

You're having an especially spectacular day. You listen to your song and hear the genius of this archetypal character you've created and fail to search for or discover ways in which you can improve on your work. This is false ego. It is also a moment of mistaken identity. That person we see ahead of us in our goals is not yet who we are. That person will always remain beyond our reach as she or he keeps stepping carefully backwards on our approach. That's the magic of goal setting. Done properly, we will never be stagnant. It's also the risk of goal setting. Done improperly, we may never feel a sense of achievement. Ideally, we'll want to punch through the board only in order to step past it, reinvent, and continue.

Compare yourself to one thing: honesty. Have you been completely honest in your delivery, in your storytelling, in your use of your skill set, in slight and simple challenges to allow yourself full expression in the now? Don't over-reach. Don't dumb it down. Is it hard? Yes. But it's always back to that self-awareness thing.

If you can develop an ability to step back and listen, you have a good chance of knowing whether this song requires some work or stands well as it is. Just to beat it in: I often will leave a new tune to sit for a week or so after I think I'm done with it. Then I'll revisit it and possibly run it by someone I trust to be truthful. For me, it's often my wife, Megan. Her honesty is one of the many things I treasure about her. I also have other musical friends who will give me straight answers if asked. When I get it in front of an audience for the first time, it's usually at an open stage. They're more forgiving and very honest in their responses, since they're under no obligation either way. Many of them tend to be other musicians, too. If they say something about your new song, you can believe them. You may want to go with the majority response for self-preservation. However, you'll want to at least give the minority report some consideration.

Be honest with who you are in this moment and what you have to say. Never, ever, ever, for any reason, compare yourself to another artist. You are a unique person with frailties, strengths, commonalities, and diversions in this world that give you this outlet and outlook. There will be enough in what you share to touch others if it is real in its presentation. There will be enough of you alive in your song to give it a proper twist and grab the listener's attention. You and the now are key to you in the future.

On The Road Again

Stories From And About The Road

In retrospect it fast becomes apparent that it's somewhat of a miracle I ever got anything done on tour. I'm a little surprised I survived, too! These often-crazy road trips were also surrounded with long periods of intense work, however. While on the road, parties aside, there was a great deal of work done by phone, especially with the onset of the smart phones in more recent years. Prior to that, I once booked an entire tour to New Mexico and back by flip phone while riding Chicago's Metra Rail to and from a teaching gig. So, I've always tried to keep up with having the right tools. Touring, in fact, is what convinced me to break down and get a new phone. I'm on my third such smarty since that technological leap. In addition to the business beyond the stage, radio, interviews, and meet-ups, it wasn't unusual for me to have someone else doing a certain amount of work for me from home, whether it was an intern, a friend, a publicist, or a girlfriend. When it's a short run, 90% of the busy work is done before hitting the road. With technology being what it is, it's great to have the ability to punch up the publicity along the way. Longer trips usually involve some break of a day or two that allows for any catching up to be done. If not, computer and phone are put to frantic use at hotels, rest stops, or wherever the opportunity presents itself. I've booked a hotel from its own parking lot using their wifi to bid online. Being a creative type and remembering that business is a creative enterprise, one finds a way to also be creative with time.

These experiences taught me a lot about touring and if I learned one huge thing from all of it, it would be the importance of planning. There were a number of times when I could have ended up completely screwed, stranded in a far away city, unable to fulfill my obligations, and well, completely screwed. It was pure luck and fast thinking that allowed me many of my little successes. I would caution anyone planning to tour the way I did to not gamble on anything. Presume you won't make any money. Presume nobody will show up at half the shows and get ready for a cancellation or two. By approaching your trip with a bit more caution, you won't be losing any of the adventure. Believe me, things will happen to test your improvisational skills as a tour manager. Trust me also, that if you enjoy travel, this may be one of the most fun ways to do it. You are truly in the heart of society and living within each cultural community. You are never a tourist. It's a blast.

Head East Young Lads

Phil and Serge close up the latter's bar in Logan Square. They walk over to Phil's building. Serge has his suitcase packed and ready for their trip. Serge breaks into the twelve-pack he brought from the bar. Phil runs upstairs to pack and grab his guitar and some merchandise (merch) to sell on tour. Phil comes back downstairs. They sit, drink beer, and chat until about 4am when Mike drives up in his old Jeep Cherokee to begin their little weekend run to the East Coast.

"Mike, how was the drive?"

"It is what it is Lad. Let's get going."

Mike insists on driving the whole way to Washington D.C. this day for a gig at 8pm... yes, today. Mike is arriving after having driven nonstop from Denver, 15 hours. Nothing could possibly go wrong. They promptly load up the luggage, beer, and gear...in that order. Serge and Phil continue to drink through Indiana (what else ya gonna do) and sleep it off through Ohio. They wake up somewhere in Pennsylvania. Mike is still alive and swilling coffee, singing to the radio, and talking to himself. It's a beautiful part of the country as they ride through the Allegheny Mountains. They're making good time.

As Phil, Mike, and Serge make their way into D.C. at around 6pm, the traffic on the beltway is pretty thick. The beltway is where Phil has always gotten turned around in the past. He'd find himself literally driving around for an hour, over and over past the same exit. As with any beltway, it circumnavigates the city. But the D.C. beltway includes the states surrounding it. And anytime a river runs through it... let's just say it all fucks with Phil's navigational skills. Chicago, his beloved hometown, is a grid. It's easy. Cities not on a grid? Phil won't drive. Nobody wants him to either. He tends to get cranky and yell at the ghosts of the founding fathers. Which means this happens pretty much everywhere he tours.

"Fuck! Maryland! Goddammit! Virginia? What stoned motherfucker laid this place out?!" Spouts Phil in some eloquence of this realm.

To avoid by distraction some such outburst on this day, Phil jumps in the backseat and pulls out his guitar to practice his tunes for this evening's show. Serge is finally driving now. Mike is so slaphappy from lack of sleep, he's in the way back wailing on his suitcase like it's a drum and banging his head like they're doing "Bohemian Rhapsody" in a Gremlin. Phil still manages to frantically bitch at the traffic in between lyrics until they make it to the house of the producer, who lives in Alexandria, Virginia. As far as Phil can tell, it's somewhere across some goddamned river out in the fucking country.

They have just enough time to clean off the road sweat and powder their noses before scrambling to the show at Madam's Organ in the Adam's Morgan neighborhood of D.C. Like the pun? Jill, the producer, first flew Phil out for some shows the year before to see how he'd come across in D.C. He did well enough. He came through another time on his way to New York and again did well. Now she's putting him on the 2nd biggest morning radio show in town... the very next morning, at 7am. Jill works for Fox Radio and News and incidentally dislikes it. She's an old hippie who goes to "Burning Man" every year. A job's a job, however, and she's great at hers.

Jill drives the whole crew, drops them at the venue, and goes to park the car. They load in, and Phil plugs and plays.

The show goes great, people buy CDs, and while Catfish Hodge, the next act, is up playing, Phil and the guys proceed to take full advantage of Phil's free drink tab. Serge is hitting tequila; Phil and Mike, being Irish, are hitting the Jameson. Serge is taken by the jelly jar glasses in which the bar serves their beer and wants to snag a few. Phil is touring the four floors of this lanky venue. Mike is staggering from fatigue and whiskey, and more or less leaning on the bar for moral support. Phil ends up trying to find company in some girl, being drunk, if not single. You'd think in four floors, an attractive (or not) guitar player could find some attention. It's usually a subtle thing, the way Phil approaches it. He's rarely been any good at pick-up lines. Phil's actually kind of shy. That's his story and he's sticking to it, because it's after all true. He's acting. Poorly.

"Hey did you catch the show tonight?"

"No, who played?"

"Oh, a couple acts. I just opened for these guys."

"What do you play?"

"Guitar and voice."

(Unintentional cheesy smile)

"I love guitar!"

41

"Me, too, that'd be why I play it."

Suddenly, Phil isn't some shaggy-looking 30-something, now he's a rock star, and then...

"What kinda music?"

This is where Phil becomes acidly sarcastic, seeing as he hates the question. It also may point at one reason why he's had fewer hook-ups. Not that that's a bad thing. He's remained disease-free. If not always drug free.

"Um, the kind with rhythm and melody."

An understandably annoyed look comes from this trixie, whose head bounces off her shoulders as she speaks. Phil doesn't understand. Still, he laughs and continues his tour of the establishment, looking for more people to observe or bother. He loves watching things unfold around him. He'll stand with his beer in hand, occasionally calling for another shot, and just scan the room. He loves the curious outlook he's sure his spirit has. He's even proud of the somewhat faulty vessel in which it's encased. From his vantage point, life is a glorious adventure. Nothing needs to be boring. If it is, he'll create a mission to make it less so. This can have its repercussions, he's found on more than one occasion.

When Phil gets back from his unfortunately uneventful explorations, Serge surreptitiously hands him and Mike each a jelly jar beer glass and says,

"Here, put these in your pants."

This seems an odd request. Nonetheless, Mike and Phil shrug and do as instructed. They all walk out past the doorman attempting to be nonchalant. As they pass the exit, Serge says,

"Let's go next door for some pizza."

Phil forgets that he's sucking in his gut to hide the beer mug and proclaims,

"Oh hell yeah, I really need some food."

The word "hell" is what vocalists call a good belt pull. The jelly jar launches out of Phil's waistline, narrowly misses his jaw and smashes on the ground right next to the doorman, who reels around like he's on point. Phil's a professional improviser. He looks up with a panicked look on his face while pointing at the upper balconies of the bar and yells,

"Holy shit, I almost got hit! Some drunk idiot dropped their fucking glass!"

After narrowly escaping the broken jelly jar glass incident outside Madam's Organ Phil, Serge, and Mike go next door for pizza. Music and people float around them. Jill is presumed lost somewhere in the venue. The guys are all lit up like Christmas trees, have no attention span, and need food. Much of this time, Mike has had his video camera rolling, if shakily. As they walk back over and stand in front of the bar eating their slices, Phil and Serge have their backs to the street while Mike films them. Jill comes up behind Phil and Serge and says,

"I'm going to get the car."

Immediately after she walks away, Phil turns to Serge and slurs,

"Hey, where's Jill?"

Serge just shrugs and keeps chewing. It's all on tape. Mike brought it up days later with a laugh. He's a consummate documentarian. He films everything, shares stories of everywhere he's been across the country and back playing music, and he loves to do all of it. *He* should write a book.

The guys decide to go inside and look for Jill. Either Mike hadn't noticed her at the time either, or chose to just come along for some more fun. The doorman won't let them back in because they are all too drunk. They glance at each other, jaws agape and trying to appear steady. Serge explains with an attempt at authority as the "tour manager" that Phil had just played in their venue earlier. The doorman shrugs with his hands out and palms up, and says with an amused smirk,

"Ahhh, no."

Then, right on cue and as if by magic, Jill pulls up with all the gear loaded; Phil, Mike, and Serge stand swaying on the sidewalk. They climb in, and everyone heads back to her place in Alexandria, where she has set up an after party. Here's hoping the pizza has slowed the effects of the alcohol.

Now in the music business, when a producer or other person of import to keeping the gates open sets up a party, you have to go. It's expected of you. It's also considered an important networking opportunity. But mainly, people in and around music on both the creative and business end, like to feel important. And they're all too happy to inform you through inference of how special they are. It goes something like this:

"Man, I was at this wicked-ass party with a touring metal band from Helsinki and we rocked it 'til dawn. The bass player guy's brother-in-law's cousin twice removed used to clean up Jimmy Page's dog's shit. It was cool."

Also, a friend of Serge's from Chicago happened to be in New York on business and was going to make the party. He took The Chinatown Bus down to D.C. for $20. Keep that in mind, should you want to make the trip. The price may have escalated, as this was 2003. But for certain, it remains affordable and is a sort of secret entryway. Bill confirmed this:

"I was the only non-Asian on the bus. It was cool."

Back to the house... Phil and Serge are nice and toasty, Mike toasty and tired from not sleeping for two days. Phil still has to be on the radio show Jill produces at 7am, with potentially a million people listening. After that, he is slated to rehearse with someone from American Idol, who is also at the party. Part of the deal with the radio is that this woman, also a previous Fox Radio guest, would get to sit in with Phil at his gig the following night, and the station would promote it.

Then, the guys have to get to New York for a show at CBGB Sunday night, and be back in Chicago no later than 11pm on Monday for yet another show.

Phil has straightened up enough to appear like he's straightened up enough and is having a great time meeting new people, hanging with his friends Mike, Serge, Jill, and the newly arrived Bill. Everything is rolling along nicely. Something has escaped Phil's attention, however. The time.

3am draws near. Phil is outside having a smoke when Mike comes out to join him. As they're standing there, Mike suddenly turns to Phil and starts berating him.

"What in the fuck is wrong with you?! Do you have any idea how much I wish *my* music would provide these opportunities for *me*?! How lucky you are to be able to tour around playing the music you've written, to make a living doing what you love?... and look at your sorry ass! You're gonna be on the radio in four hours with like a million people listening! What are you doing? You're partying away like it's no big fucking deal! I won't have anything to do with it! I won't be held responsible! Fuck this shit!"

Mike spins around and violently opens the back of his Cherokee. He angrily yanks out Phil's gear and plops it on the sidewalk in front of him. Phil barely even has time to respond, standing there completely dumbfounded. As Mike is slamming his door and speeding away, Phil manages to get out (with something of the voice of Milton from *Office Space*),

"Um, but Mike, I didn't know, um, I, uh…"

He shakes his head in disbelief and, trying not to panic, grabs his gear and takes it inside where Serge glances at him and asks,

"Where's Mike?"

"Um," Phil stutters, "he just drove away. Apparently, he's, uh, a bit upset."

Phil still looks like a deer in headlights. Jill chimes in from the middle of another conversation,

"And I can't drive you to the show, you know I have to be there in two hours."

Bill chimes in,

"Well, I grabbed a rental after I got off the bus in China Town. I can get us all there. What time do we have to get up?"

(Fuck me)

"In three hours."

Bill gets directions from Jill so they can find the radio station. Phil is about to have a coronary because he's convinced they'll get lost. Being still drunk and exhausted during the show doesn't seem to phase him. But it's more likely that it simply hasn't occurred to him. Everyone is trying to be reassuring.

"You'll make the show."

"Don't sweat it."

"There's this new thing called Mapquest."

That being generally handled there is still no idea as to where Mike went or if he is coming back. There remains the question of how to get to New York for the following night's performance, to say nothing of getting home to Chicago. Phil crawls into bed and slumps to sleep.

It seems minutes later. It's 6am. Phil, Bill, and Serge are up and moving. Mike is still not answering his cell. Everyone has been heartily run over by the previous night's activities, seeing as they only just ended. Phil has an hour before he has to be interviewed and play live on a major radio network with the entire D.C. metro area within earshot. Bill and Serge hoist Phil into Bill's rental, and they head to the radio show.

In the Green Room, waiting to be called into the studio, they pour water and coffee down Phil's throat, washing down donuts and various pastries. He sits and warms up his guitar and rather hoarse and tired voice in the process. Then, Jill comes in and tells him it's time. He glances back at Bill and Serge with a look of terror on his face. They both wave him on with encouraging looks.

"You'll tear it up, brother!"

"Go get 'em!"

Phil and Jill walk down the hallway to what he feels may be his potential doom. He often feels like he might die right before an appearance of this (perceived) level of importance. He's often suffered from stage fright. This morning it's more like outright stage terror.

His fear would tend to work in his favor, however. With the feeling of nothing to lose, he would let go completely. With the typical luck of the Irish, Phil pulled it off. Somehow, his feeling of helplessness drove him to an outstanding and unhindered performance of his songs, and a lively interview.

Jill had warned Phil that the host wasn't the brightest bulb in the pack and may ask some dumb questions, but to just go with it. Phil played his tune "Down to the Sea." It's about environmental issues and was inspired by his learning that the Colorado River and Rio Grande die in the sand before they hit the ocean. Phil's music doesn't usually lean this way. But this tune does, and it seems to be popular with people that know his work.

After the song, the host says,

"That was fantastic! So, what sea in particular is that about?"

Phil tries not to laugh as he sees Jill in the control room

with her face in her hands, and explains the premise of the song.

More questions lacking profundity follow. Phil tries to make the answers more thoughtful in hopes of helping out. The host really was a nice guy, just not the most clever as far as interviewers go. Phil plays a few more songs, and the show eventually wraps up with the host saying,

"We've had singer/songwriter/guitarist Phil Circle on the show this morning. This guy is a virtuosic guitar player, he writes profound lyrics, and boy, does he have a voice."

And to his credit, the host had that voice, too. Perfect for radio. (Of course I think this... he liked me!)

Victory. Phew.

Phil feels great; praise from anybody hits his heart. And a show of such magnitude is important to getting one's name out. Yes, there's that pesky business and promotions angle popping up its ugly head. When one is an independent musician, one needs to take every opportunity, as long as it doesn't go against his or her mores. Performing music in any sort of venue rarely goes against Phil's grain. It's his favorite moment. He's happy. Others are happy. It's like a divine selfishness.

When they've all returned to the house in Alexandria, Phil crawls back into bed giving little thought to what's next. At about 11am, Bill comes in and rouses him.

"Phil, Mike's back."

Phil gets up gingerly and comes out, apologizing his way through the door for being so reckless night before. Mike sloughs it off on his part as a reaction brought on by sleep deprivation. All he had done after his rant was drive around the corner, park, and crash until minutes ago. All appears good again.

Shortly, the American Idol contestant shows up to run through the couple songs she'll be singing with Phil's guitar accompaniment at that night's gig. The partying begins early, but this time it also ends early. Mike, Serge, Phil, and Bill are all off to New York City the following morning for Phil's show at the legendary and now defunct CBGB in The Bowery. This will be his second appearance there. They'd asked him back after his first one, which also had a hand in spurring this trip.

As Mike and Serge trade driving duties on the road to New York, Phil naps in the back, intermittently waking up to crack a beer and practice for the show. Bill has gone on in his rental car to continue with the business he was out here to do.

They arrive with plenty of time to get settled into The Avalon, a classy old hotel from about the 1920s that sits under the shadow of The Empire State Building. Phil's publicist had gotten the room online for $100, a steal for anything in Manhattan. The room has a bed, a couch, and the floor; where Phil, Serge and Mike all sleep, respectively.

While Serge and Phil take the gear up to the room, Mike goes to park... no easy task. However, it is no time at all before Mike comes parading through the door.

"Found a spot right out front, but I have to move by 9am or it gets towed."

"We'll get up early," Phil hopes.

They all relax for a while, drinking beer and smoking cigarettes with the window open. The room is non-smoking. It comes time to head to the gig. They each grab a piece of equipment and all take the elevator to the lobby where the concierge hails a cab. They head to the venue.

Phil pulls off another successful show and meets a reviewer who has come by. She responds positively to his performance and seems to enjoy the variety and mix of styles. She ends up reviewing some future CD releases of Phil's over the years. They remain in touch to this day. He's back in Chicago. She's in Memphis with her girlfriend.

After the show, the guys all hang out in front of CBGB for a while, talking with patrons and passersby. Hunger sets in again. Finding food at 2am in "the city that never sleeps" is not a tall order. They grab a cab back to the hotel to leave off the gear.

While in the cab, Mike announces from the front passenger seat that it is now officially his birthday and he is ready to keep the party going. Neither Phil nor Serge had known. Mike asks the Lebanese cab driver where they could find food, beer, and women. All are very important ingredients for one's birthday festivities. The cabby explains that he had been a concierge at a high-class hotel in Lebanon.

"Ask your concierge, he'll tell you all you need to know."

When they get to the hotel, Mike leaves the other guys to haul the gear to the elevator while he slips the concierge a wad of cash and starts asking questions. As the elevator doors open, Mike is heading for the front exit yelling,

"Guys, I'll be right back!"

They shrug and load into the elevator. About twenty minutes later, a knock comes on the door to their room. Phil opens it to see Mike trying to steady several six-packs of beer and a bunch of Chinese food.

"There's a 24-hour Chinese joint around the corner, and if you ask them for some beer, they'll pull as much as you want out of their cooler in back. Even after hours! Oh, and there're a bunch of girls partying on the seventh floor!"

Everyone acts as if this is normal, and the party goes on into the wee hours. As the T.V. buzzes, they sit telling stories and jokes, swilling beer and puffing away. Serge relates their last trip to D.C. and New York, which Mike wasn't on. Mike talks about traveling all summer after his Dad passed away. Phil jumps in here and there. They all have a good ole time; the early morning passes uneventfully; they never make it to the seventh floor.

Then...

Phil wakes up, looks at the alarm. 10:30. He rubs his eyes and squints. Still 10:30. Shit! He jumps up while frantically pulling his boots on, runs out the door like it's downhill, barely catches an elevator, and bolts clumsily out the front of the hotel... Mike's Cherokee is gone. Phil recounts what Mike said last night, retraces that this is where he pointed out he was parked, almost doesn't want to look at the sign by the empty spot. Tow Zone, 9am to 5pm. Fuckin' hell. He drudges up to the room in no way looking forward to telling Mike.

"Fiddly-dee, lad! I've never been to the Port Authority. Let's get a cab!"

So, Mike spends the day with Phil rescuing his truck from the auto pound. They spend an hour or two getting there, paying the fines, then riding in a small tram with an endless train of open carts snaking along behind it. This mini human freight ride is driven by a hefty uniformed woman with unusually long, multi-colored fingernails. Mike makes his usual bouncy conversation with her. Of course he points out her nails! She's amiable, though, and seems to enjoy someone being nice for a change. They travel what feels like miles through unfortunate rows of dusty cars in the damp, cavernous and smelly garage. After a long conversation between Mike and the driver, they finally arrive at the Cherokee. Phil and

Mike head back to the hotel to pick up Serge, the luggage, and the gear.

Phil says languidly,

"Sorry you had to spend your birthday at the Port Authority."

Mike says brightly,

"No worries, lad! I got to spend my birthday in New York City! And I can say I saw the Port Authority!"

The three of them make record time back to Chicago through serious thunderstorms, made more frightening by the bat-outa-hell driving of Serge. After a solid twelve hours, they pull up to Subterranean for Phil to go in and play. He leaps out with his guitar, jogs in, receives a shot from his waiting publicist/girlfriend (she texted she was waiting), and goes straight to the stage to cheers from the waiting crowd. Thus ends a four-day tour. A four-day tour.

Mike has been a busker all his adult life and made a living doing so. He was a regular for a long time in the Chicago subways and could be counted on to show up at any number of open stages. His secret is to have a vast list of material, his own take on all of it, and to throw his entire life into each and every performance. His repertoire is amazing. His interpretations are from the heart. He moved to Colorado.

Phil was booked for a songwriters-in-the-round show. This is where four songwriters line up across a stage. Each plays one song at a time in rotation for the duration of the show. While one artist plays, others may join in, but there's no obligation.

Phil goes to check in, and the woman who runs the thing waves him off without speaking, as she gossips with a friend of hers. He shrugs and walks away until she's free.

Joining Megan (his wife-to-be) and Matteo (a fellow musician and groomsman-to-be) at a table just below the left side of the stage from the audience perspective, they order a round of beers and shots. The server brings them, they pay, and she walks away. Matteo protests loudly:

"These cost HOW MUCH?!"

He glances out the window over his left shoulder.

"I'll be right back."

Phil and Megan watch with curiosity as he makes a beeline across the street to a liquor store. They stare at the shots politely awaiting their consumption. Five or so minutes later, Matteo's back at the table. They all happily clink and knock back their drinks after the obligatory arms-length examination. Matteo pulls a pint of some cheap-ass liquor from his jacket pocket and proceeds to refill the shot glasses... in plain sight. Now Phil protests:

"Matteo, watch it man, you know ya can't bring in outside liquor to a bar!"

Matteo laughs as he glances around with a soft smirk.

"Relax, Felipe."

He responds, however, by keeping the glasses below the rim of the table from then on.

Showtime arrives. Phil has finally caught the host when she isn't standing around apparently feeling or acting important... or, well, she's at least free for a minute.

She places him far stage right, right above the table where Megan and Matteo remain. The songwriters are ordered left to right, so Phil is last in the rotation. When it comes to be his turn, he launches into his blues tune "Pass Me Another." Matteo's voice can be heard as he leans over to Megan.

"Look at those guys' faces. They're terrified. They know Phil is kicking their asses, that he's got what they don't."

The rotation continues.

A few runs through the line-up of songwriters on stage at this hotel bar stage in Nashville, Megan and Matteo are still sitting, knocking back their drinks. While awaiting the next song by Phil, Matteo gets impatient:

"If I hear one more fucking country ballad, I'm gonna shoot myself," he says, not so quietly.

Phil hears and chuckles nervously. His turn comes. He plays his song "Lipstick and Whiskey." It's a country ballad. A couple other guys on the stage try to join in, with unfortunately little success. Odd, it's an easy tune. But this is also why Phil makes no efforts at joining the others on their songs. It's more about each song coming across to the audience than any one songwriter looking good against the others. If you jump in and can't catch the key right away or find the groove, you look lesser and take away from the song at the same time. Better to let each song stand alone. Better to let the audience not be distracted by egos. At least, this is Phil's thought, and so he remains silent except to politely applaud the others.

Eventually, the show comes to an end. Phil nonchalantly unplugs and leaves the stage to put away his guitar. A few audience members compliment him as he walks through the bar, to which he responds in a gracious manner: a "thank you" with his hand to his heart. One person asks for a CD, another asks where they can find him, etc. One woman, seeing his jean jacket with "Taylor" embroidered on the front pocket, asks if he plays for Taylor Swift. He chuckles (politely, he hopes) and explains Taylor is also a guitar manufacturer. Guess she hadn't seen the huge guitar on the back or bothered to read the smaller word, "guitars." No harm. She seemed excited anyway.

He tries to spark conversation with the other songwriters. One cordially compliments Phil's work. This same guy happened to be the only guy whose songs Phil really found really stuck out to his ears. Sometimes, too similar styles start to blend into one voice.

He talks to another and asks him if there are any open mics going on that night and gets blown off without a word.

He then speaks with another guy and suggests they connect online, as Phil is coming back through in July and would like some tips for more gigs. He gets this response:

"Yeah, man, I don't USE the internet. I have better things to do, like focus on my music."

(Um, okay.)

A bartender at another gig in Nashville said this to Phil as he swaggered around schlepping drinks:

"Yeah, I'm a writer for this music magazine, yeah, and I've got, like these two songs I wrote. I'm just waiting for one of them to hit big and I'm outa here."

"Best of luck and more power to ya," thought Phil.

Given how rare that kind of success is, it might be worth the trouble to write a few more songs before getting one's hopes up. There are successful songwriters still working outside the industry just for something to do. Self importance or ego based in one's specific work is not a healthy way to go… for oneself or the people in the immediate vicinity.

At that same gig, the sound engineer decided not to show up because she picked up a better paying job earlier that day. Megan ended up running sound for everyone instead… for free. Fortunately, their friend Donna Frost was one of the other acts, and in fact booked the evening. From what promised to be a disaster came a great evening of music between friends.

This was the unfortunate and standard impression Phil got while in Nashville: lots of musicians acting very special. And it wasn't as if there was a shortage of talent around, so no one individual was a commodity by any means. Maybe Phil was just attracting them, who can say? He had hoped for something that would counter the testimonials he had heard from other touring acts over the years about this famous music city. R'ichards, just outside of town, turned out to be one exception. Phil and Megan played there on a return trip. The owner and clientele were welcoming, as were the other musical acts. Maybe Phil was just used to the generally friendly and supportive environment he grew up on in Chicago? It's hard to say, and everything warrants another look. Phil's been through Nashville more than once and expects to return.

One key element that Donna Frost has understood and worked effectively for years: you build things in each town. You develop a respectable network of friends, musicians, and fans wherever you go. You do it by being a welcoming heart, by stowing any false ego or sense of being any more than someone else. You make sure that you thank everyone the next day, literally or figuratively. Donna is genuine and passionate about her life's work. She's been at it longer than most and hasn't lost her love for it. She seems to have a calm tolerance for the business end of things and has embraced technologies that didn't exist for the first 30 years of her career.

Weather Report

Phil is driving southwest on Interstate 44 by Rolla, Missouri. He's on his way to Springfield, where he'll stay for the night with his brother Bob, before heading the rest of the way to New Mexico for some shows. It's the middle of May.

It's 6pm, and the sky has quickly turned black with clouds. It looks like nighttime. Shortly, the wind picks up considerably, sending his little black Mazda careening back and forth. Then he sees a wall of rain heading towards him. When he collides with it, the noise is monstrous. With the wipers at full throttle, it still is nearly impossible to see, and he slows to about 25mph. Cars and trucks are pulling over into the grass along the interstate, but he determines to keep moving forward. A bright flash behind him, he peers into the rearview squinting to discern what caused it. It's a truck signaling him. The truck pulls around him and flashes his brake lights... "Follow me," in highway language.

He focuses on the taillights of the semi's trailer, and this keeps him on the road and moving forward through what can only be compared to what it must be like to drive underwater. He switches on the radio.

"And for the weather this evening... there's a chance of rain..."

(No shit.)

Must be a pre-programmed station.

Phil scans for another.

Tree branches fly across the highway between him and the truck... sideways with a major gust of wind that nearly sends his old car off the road. He steadies it, hands turning white from his death grip on the wheel. He begins talking aloud to himself.

"Awww shit. I saw *Twister*, this can't be good."

Some twisting of knobs and a live radio station is found. A properly excited Missouri accent is heard.

"Tornadoes are touching down in several towns in LaClede County along I-44 folks. If you're on the highway, pull over and get into a ditch for safety."

"And be a sitting target? No fucking way," says Phil to the radio, "and fuck! Where the hell is LaClede County?!"

He looks quickly at the clock while trying to stay steady and on the road. It seems like forever, but it's only been a little more than a half hour since the rain started. Then, an eternal five minutes pass. The rain and wind stop just as abruptly as they began. The dark and tumbling clouds remain. It's an eerie, green-tinged darkness. A dull flashing from somewhere inside the car catches his eye. He jerks his head back and forth in shallow turns and finds it's the gas gauge. An orange "E" is blinking at him with a quiet laugh.

He speaks out loud again.

"I sure as hell hope there's an exit soon with a gas station."

Ten trembling miles down the highway and there is one. Phil pulls off the exit to the right, to the top of the ramp, left across a bridge, and coasts in next to a pump. Safe. He fills up and goes in to pay. The sky in every direction hovers and rumbles frighteningly. He greets the attendant.

"Hey, what county are we in?"

"LaClede."

Time stops for a second. The attendant speaks again.

"Where ya drivin'?"

"Just came down from Rolla."

"I'll be damned, that's where them tornadoes was crossing the freeway."

If this were a movie, this would be the moment when a camera would zoom in to Phil's bugged out eyes with a tight spot on them. The attendant grins and speaks again.

"Where ya headed?"

"Springfield."

"Hear it's even worse down thereabouts. Biggest tornado storm we seen in decades. (Incidental music) We're closin' up after you leave. Goin' home to watch the twisters."

Interesting sport, thinks Phil, not knowing if the guy is joking.

Phil tries to act nonchalant, but probably stutters a "thanks" to the man. He heads out to the car and through his jitters gets back behind the wheel. He eases back onto the interstate. As he comes around the first bend with a tinge of hope, there, off to the left, he sees it. A long black rope twisting like a serpent dancing down from the clouds. The self talk continues with genuine fear in the timbre of his voice.

"I sure as fuck hope this road turns the other way!"

It did. But the relative time it took to get the relative distance required to see he had made a relative turn away from the twister was relatively excruciating.

During the next hour or so, he makes it through the return of driving rain, battering wind, and misplaced tree limbs. He has called his brother Bob from his flip phone and is being guided in. They're both yelling through the noise of the storm. Phil makes it safely through flooded streets to Bob's place in Springfield.

He walks into the house. There are hugs hello. His legs feel like he's been on a ship for the last three hours. His brother's wife Cherri says, "We have left over pizza and some juice."

Bob takes one good look at Phil, who's just realizing the aftershock of what he's been driving through. Bob says,

"You wanna get a beer?"

Phil makes several short and fast nods through his shaky nerves. His mouth is somewhat agape and eyes are drooping on the sides from distress.

Bob turns to his wife as he grabs his car keys from the kitchen counter. He kisses her and says,

"Don't wait up."

Phil's List Of Touring Cars And What Happened

The Little Red Datsun: Traded for a new car...

The 1987 Little Brown Nissan: Blew a piston straight through the hood on I-9O coming home from a job. It was going to be an early arrival home that day, until there was an explosion and lots of billowing black smoke.

The Little Blue Mazda: Totaled it running into the back of an RV trailer that had no brake lights hooked up. The other driver dropped Phil and his stuff off in Albuquerque. The car stayed in the ditch for a wrecking company in Tucumcari to pick up.

The Big Blue Chevy: Sold it, gas was too much and food was needed. Should've traded it for a microphone instead.

The Little Green Fiat: First wife (there were two before Megan) made him sell it and get a more practical car...

The Little Silver Subaru: Kept breaking down, so the mechanic got him into another one...

The Little Red Ford: Gave it back to the mechanic and got...

The Little Red Rusty Volvo for $400: Got booted for $1500 in outstanding Chicago parking tickets. Slipped the guy at the auto pound $20 to get in and grab all the music gear from the trunk. Left the car.

The Big Green Limousine: The CTA still runs every day of the year and will get you by bus or train to just about anywhere in Chicago day or night. This became less relied upon due to picking up...

The Little Black Nissan: Handed it over to a long-time friend for his oldest son to drive, in exchange for money owed. This happened when The Little Blue Honda drove into Phil's life with Megan at the wheel.

She pulled up slowly, a pair of Hepburn shades on, the blonde waves of her hair dusting her long neck in the breeze. Her lips gave a subtle pseudo kiss as she played with the collar of her low cut blouse. Then she whispered in that sultry voice, "Want a ride, old man?"

I glanced down past the upturned collar of my newly dry cleaned pea coat and examined her through my tinted prescription bifocals. Pulling the cigarette from my mouth as I turned my head to meet her gaze, I smirked slightly and said,

"Yeah, alright," while trying not to cough from the smoke wreathing me like a dragon's breath.

Okay, it didn't happen quite like that. We met at The Chicago Actors Studio when she started classes there and I was teaching out of the prop room.

She floated past me like Lauren Bacall...

And the last...

The Little Blue Honda: Put out to pasture with 240,000 miles on it. It needed $6-800 worth of work and was worth $50. We gave it to the mechanic for an oil change on the Little Red Chevy. That was early 2016.

Where It Began, I Can't Begin To Know It

In 2003, Megan Corse bought a used car at Ken Vance Honda in Eau Claire, Wisconsin. Even past 200,000 miles, it still got upwards of 30mpg. Ken Vance gave us magnetic signs for the car... and Phil Circle coached Ken's adult son Jason Vance in voice. He also accompanied Jason at his sister's wedding. That's when Phil met Ken Vance, himself. Nice guy. He sure liked his scotch. So did Phil.

In early 2008, Megan started classes at The Chicago Actors Studio. By April we were dating. In the late summer we drove in her Honda to New Mexico to see if we could stand each other for twenty-four hours a day on the road for a week.

On the way back, I asked her how she thought it was went. She responded with an almost unnoticeable twinkle in her eye:

"I'll let you know when we get home."

When we arrived home, I moved in with her. That was August. Thus began my life with Megan and her little blue Honda Civic.

July 15th, 2010. Megan and Phil have shoved everything they can into a storage unit in Chicago, stocked the Honda with all they can fit in gear and supplies, and left the rest behind at the apartment. The landlord, who knew they were leaving, called and asked about the remaining items. Phil told him he could have them... a computer and mountain bike were included. They hoped he made out well. They owed him back rent.

They had taken shifts to rest all night, of about an hour each until it was time to leave. On limited sleep, they made their way to the first gig in Louisville, Kentucky. Megan often had a look of horror on her face much of the time until they eventually hit Beale St. in Memphis and then Bourbon St. in New Orleans. These locations made any hardship or fear pretty much go away. It was becoming truly exciting. Megan had done very little traveling until recently. On one trip with Phil she would add something like 10 states to her list of "been there."

Optimism and thrills don't pay bills. By Gainesville, Florida, they had $6 left. Wondering if they'd have to sleep in the car, Megan double-checked the bank account and saw that someone had donated $100 to the tour. The donor added a note:

"Here's some money to help with the tour. Keep it up! I'm living vicariously through you guys."

This wasn't their first trip in the old blue Honda. But it was on this trip that "The Little Blue Honda Tour" became synonymous with skating by from town to town and playing shows that were often lightly attended. It happened that someone else who sent money along the way commented on "the little Blue Honda" in a message of encouragement. It stuck because Phil began using it on every trip thereafter.

The Little Blue Honda Tour

I came very close to starting this narration with the words "where do I start?" Having narrowly averted this time-tested writer's cliché...if only by entering the same parking spot via the alley...and then following it with a shaky metaphor that lands a bit too close to my topic, I have thereby accomplished a first paragraph, book-ended with annoying meta-bits and a run-on sentence that may cause you to stop reading.

Good, you didn't.

Good, you still didn't.

My wonderfully supportive and lovely fiancé (at the time of this writing) Megan introduced me to a thing they do in film known as non-linear. I promptly realized how much I enjoy the confusion and frenetic fun to be had in trying to follow the spaghetti strands of this approach. I also realized how often I've incorporated it into my writing. I tried it with music, but found out that a first verse just didn't work as a third chorus or bridge, so I'll leave non-linear music to all the John Cage students.

I start from where I sit. In this instance, I'm on a floor in a remarkably non-ergonomic position between two beds. Please, for those of the more singularly polished rails of the mind, take note that I'm sitting and writing...not kneeling before someone or hanging from a harness powered by propane. I'm participating in a short break from an ongoing tour performing solo sets of music wherever anyone will allow me to. By short break, I mean I'm sitting here at 3am Mountain Daylight Time (so, I'm not in Arizona), following several hours of work online. Okay, so I'm online now aspiring to this bit of story telling... if I ever get around to it. My partner, in life and crime, and I just drove nine hours from Oklahoma City. She is sitting enjoying some "down time" submitting my music to music site #437. She's trying, anyway. Right now she's swearing at a slow browser.

We're in Albuquerque, New Mexico, staying with a friend. There are no gigs booked for me currently. This is the break part. It won't last long. By Friday, that's tomorrow if I just stay up, I'll have another show booked. I can't remember the last time I've looked at my calendar and seen no gigs on it, though. There's always been at least one or two, and only so few because I may have been busy playing five in eight days previous to that. That's when time spent focused on booking is practically non-existent. Last minute promoting, and musical preparation, aka practice, become more important. It feels strange, almost empty, especially when my wallet (okay, front right pocket, I hate wallets ever since being rolled for $350 on the "L" in Chicago) is also empty. But I know why it is: I'm on the road. They don't know me everywhere. In fact, they hardly know me anywhere. This is hopefully being partially remedied. This thing I do really doesn't usually feel like work. Here's a sample of the laid back schedule of the rock star gypsy traipsing from town to town:

July 15th Megerz (Megan) and I hit the road in our Little Blue Honda for what was originally expected to be a 30-day run of shows (it keeps growing). It's now August 11th. We've stopped and visited and in some cases slept in 23 different cities, I've played 20 or more sets of music. We've visited Thomas Jefferson's home Monticello; drank on Beale St. and Bourbon St. (sure and 23 other streets and avenues); experienced the joyous adventure of a fishing boat's engine overheating right before noon in the middle of the Everglades during the hottest summer in years; seen many old friends and family, made many new ones; got lost twice in Manhattan (who hasn't, right?); failed to stop at all the Civil War battlefields I wanted to see; learned how having oil in your car's engine can really help with gas mileage (and how a Honda can still drive without it); became extremely creative with living frugal and still managed to get into nice hotels for less than $45 by booking online the night before or even the day of; and we have successfully filled a couple one-gallon zip-lock bags with condiments from truck stops and the complimentary toiletries from hotels. All of this we've managed while still continuing the booking and promotion process. Sound fun? It is! We are now looking at how far we can push this. The road has proven a happy place for us (it's like our bliss, dude). What this tour of two artists, two guitars, and a year 2000 model car with 138,800 miles on it, jammed with supplies, has turned into is becoming a bit mind-boggling.

We're documenting the trip through words (ours and those of people we've seen on the road, maybe you if you're nice), pictures (Megan is going through hundreds of them as I write this, she moved on from the uncooperative browser), and of course, video. I'm a little afraid of what she may edit into final form on that last medium. I get kind of nuts every time I have to drive across the mind-numbingly flat Texas panhandle, and today the camera was on from Amarillo to Tucumcari.

I'm An Air Conditioned Gypsy In A Little Blue Honda

I'm back in New Mexico. It's July of 2010.

Thomas Wolfe was wrong. Or at the very least, was wrought with two afflictions: the positive-minded vigor of Eeyore or Gollum, and the lack of a thesaurus that defines home as more than an abode or a series of isolated childhood incidents. You can go home again. Done it, did it, got it, good.

I left my new home in New Mexico in 1992. After nine

months of travel that took me back through for short intervals, I finally landed back in my hometown of Chicago. Since then, I've returned to The Southwest a dozen or more times. I've flown two or three times. When driving, I always come in from the east on I-40 over Tijeras Pass between the Sandia and Manzano Mountains, save one occasion when I entered by way of El Paso (from the south). I usually take the shorter stretch on day two from Oklahoma City, but have on the more ambitious drives come straight through from somewhere like Joplin, Missouri. As I come around that final bend through the shaded long and rolling pass, and see the lights of Albuquerque spreading out before me like a thousand stationary fireflies in formation, I always feel that I've returned home.

While I was born and raised in Chicagoland and have spent the better part of my life there, it was my growth as a young man, that good old coming-of-age and finding-of-one's-purpose, that made New Mexico so much like my new chosen home. When I was a teenager, my Pops was always taking me out of town with him on business trips, always hoping to keep me away from my relentless troublemaking back in Chicago. It was on one such trip that I found myself sitting atop Sandia's crest overlooking Albuquerque from 10,800 feet. It was 1983, the year my wife was born. I was seventeen. I wanted to move here. I became obsessed. I bought all kinds of Southwest-style accouterments in belts, jewelry, a hat, some cowboy boots. I read all about the history of the area, what living there was like, what the music was like.

73

Five years later my opportunity came. After an especially debilitating illness in late 1988 that left me unable to work full time, and doctor's "orders" to find a more favorable climate, I sold all that wouldn't fit into my brother's red pick-up and made the move. On March 28th, 1989, my brother drove away, leaving me and my small belongs and a stash of cash at The Royal Hotel on Central Avenue... next to the adult bookstore, in Albuquerque. By the end of the week, I was playing my first gig in their lounge. Through the Buddhist organization I've been a part of since 1986, I found several new friends at the local community center. They took on the job of escorting me about town to various destinations. While they were mostly bars, there were a few restaurants and strip clubs on the list, as well. They took me to five or six destinations a night for five nights. It was very enlightening. Several of these guys are friends to this day.

Although I'd played shows back in Chicago, I really started pursuing my music career more seriously in Albuquerque. Life threatening illness had concocted in me a profound and almost blind desire to see music as my absolute only long-term career choice.

I experienced impending respiratory failure after pushing myself too hard for an entire summer, triggering a dangerous attack of my asthma. The doctors had me intubated and drugged to a level that would lead to cardiac arrest if they added more. They literally told me it was up to me to survive and wheeled me into intensive care for the night. My parents sent in their parish priest, Joe Mazza, probably to offer last rites. I couldn't speak, but wrote a note:

"Father Mazza, I think it's wonderful that you would come in here to see me, knowing I'm a practicing Buddhist. It truly shows that you are more than the parish priest, but a family friend. Please come back tomorrow when I can speak. Thank you."

He looked confused as to what he should do, how he should respond. He honored my request and left.

As I fought for each breath through the feeling of crushing gravity imploding my fragile chest, my girlfriend said through tears:

"Don't die."

I hadn't thought about this prospect! I was so busy just fighting I had no time to consider success or failure and the consequences of either. Now, I asked myself. What if I die? A strange feeling hit me accompanied by the ongoing internal chant of my Buddhist mantra, nam-myoho-renge-kyo. If I died right now, it was okay. I was only twenty-two. I hadn't accomplished shit. I wasn't the greatest guy. I had a lot to learn. I had a lot I wanted to do. But, it would be okay. Death isn't an end. From there, elation filled me. I was sitting up the next morning talking to Joe Mazza about world religions and chatting about life in general. I knew my time wasn't to be wasted on anything outside music.

So, it was 1989. I worked various odd jobs for food and rent until landing additional income working with an audio technician. We installed the sound system in downtown Albuquerque's Kimo Theater, among other locations. He and his partner brought with them plenty of experience in the world of music. One had worked at The Power Station in New York. The other had worked with the likes of Stevie Ray and Jimmy Lee Vaughan and Edie Brickell, in Austin. Through their tutelage, I learned about music production. On our downtime they threw CD after CD on (a new technology at the time). They would point out the stylistic moves of the artists, how the producers worked to develop the sound of the album, where their ideas may have come from, and what the studio tricks were that they used. One album sticks in my ear to this day. It's John Lee Hooker's album "The Healer." I love this album.

I also immersed myself further in the practice of Buddhism and became very attached to a large community of Buddhists, many of whom still live in Albuquerque.

One of the guys I met at the time who has remained a dear friend to this day now resides in Chicago. Our differing political views and his ridiculous intelligence and knowledge of things have always made for challenging debates. Had we been judged, I would've lost. After many a night of tequila shots and hurling around facts to back our stances, we'd marvel how our interaction was the benchmark of a

Democracy. The next day I'd run to research all the shit he said that stumped me, in omniscient preparation for our next meeting. This same guy once told me not to use a band name. He explained that whatever group I put together, we'd inevitably be playing my music and I'd no doubt end up running the band. He felt that justified any group I formed just being called "Phil Circle" whatever the line-up. He also stood next to me one evening looking out along the Chicago River downtown shortly after he moved there. He gestured widely, creating an arm reach sweep over the sight of the buildings standing guard along the banks and in his Italian accent said,

"Phil, man. Look at this beautiful city. This is you, man! You are Chicago. You belong here, not anywhere else!"

I believe he was right on both counts.

While later working a "regular" job by The University of New Mexico, I became friends with a couple of longhaired rockers. I bought a cassette duplicator and some blanks through my friend the audio guy and ended up making some extra cash doing a short run of demos for them. The first mosh pit I experienced was at a loosely thrown together "concert" at a junkyard in the North Valley where my two fellow workers' band played a set. I soon got my first tattoo, probably as result of being surrounded by inked-up people. It cost $25 from a guy named "Tattoo Tom" and was done in a converted garage somewhere in a sketchy neighborhood. I didn't catch anything.

I now have five tats.

The music scene at that time was made up of retired and neo-hippies playing in foggy jam bands, Norteños, Country musicians, and a new and burgeoning hard rock scene. Occasionally, rap would crop up. The other night, as Megan and I pulled through Tijeras Pass on the way to stay with our friend Karen, I wondered how the scene has changed.

After a long day of intermittently sitting inside or out, reading about the Irish (Karen is one of us), writing about my travels, practicing and promoting, Megan and I were invited to a party on the West Side of Albuquerque, hosted by friends we met at Karen's "Leo Party" on our previous trip.

As I drove us up the hill towards the West Mesa, the sun was setting behind the Three Sisters--dormant volcanoes that formed the mesa 40,000 years ago. The wispy remnants of evening rain clouds left their droplets evaporating in mid-air, refracting colors everywhere with a perfect cobalt blue sky as a backdrop. Behind us, across the valley, the sunlight filtering through the airborne desert dust splashed the mountains in a red hue that made it easy to see why the Spaniards named them the Sandia and Manzano; "watermelon" and "apple" in Spanish. As we pulled up to the party, a gibbous moon alighted in the darkening sky to the west with one companion star.

"Oh my god," gasped Megan, "this is absolutely beautiful. If there was anything for us here, I'd move in a second."

"Well," I responded, "every day, the people of New Mexico are rewarded for their forbearance in a weaker economy with fewer jobs, by the beauty of the land. And every night, the Gods give them the bonus of a painting across the sky that even the greatest artist would be hard put to emulate."

She nodded slowly, eyes bright, and said "Amen."

The party was mostly stationed in a garage. Our friend Alex and his musical contemporaries were listening intermittently to Reggae and Hip-hop while using their dilapidated T-shirt press (only two of the six presses still worked) to print up shirts for their show Saturday in Denver. T's hung everywhere drying the group's name, Government Cheese, into their fabric. As the Jameson flowed and curious pungent smells floated about, they spread ink onto the next piece of merchandise while free-style rapping over the music. In time, discussions of the state of music turned to impassioned debates directed at the outside world, on how to implement change in the industry …and life. Music and life... huh, somehow related, they are. Megan kept the video camera running, the shots kept coming. We broke for vegetarian lasagna (Alex is also a professional chef), and the music and discussion continued until Megan, Karen, and her daughter and I returned to the North Valley to retire for the evening.

As I stood under the night sky, I pondered our experience. I began working through the thoughts that have become a blog and came to this: Home is not a location. Most people will say that. And the spirit of home is not the initial experience we had as youth per se. It is more the nature of that experience. The music may have changed, but the spirit of it has not. Our lives evolve. So many times I stood outside a party with friends, somewhere in Albuquerque between 1989 and 1992, drinking, listening to music, and thinking out loud at each other as we searched for our place and purpose in life. In so many places, this continues today. And as such, home is still here for me where this spirit began and grew when I was 23. You can. That's your answer. You can return home. You can keep the spirit of your youth. Thomas Wolfe was mistaken.

The Refried Little Honda Azul

Just past Abilene en-route to Austin, we're moving with a fair amount of uncertainty. Upon arrival in Austin, apart from a few dimes left on the credit cards and in Megan's purse, we will have no countable amount of cash. We're waiting for a couple of transfers to come through online, but need money now for a hotel room, gas, and food... you know the small shit. Don't sweat the small stuff? Fuck that, we need the small stuff now. Maybe we can manage the food, we'll split another sub or something. Gas? Well, we can use a credit card. It only puts a $1 hold on it until the full transaction goes through the system and posts. But the hotel! Crap. We may be making a reservation for our backseat... if only it weren't full of gear and luggage.

We pull over to a hotel along the road somewhere in

Brownwood, Texas. In our car in their parking lot, Megan pulls out her laptop and checks to see if their WiFi is secure. It isn't. Sweet. We use it to get online and hit Priceline to start bidding on hotels in Austin. It has to come to less than $42 with taxes and fees (which usually run about $12 a night). Our first few tries don't work... the amount is too high and the card is refused. She does some clever workaround that fools the site into thinking we're making a completely new bid. The computer starts beeping. The battery is dying! It's plugged into the adaptor in the car, but it turns out it runs too high a wattage for the car to handle. $25? Rejected. Resubmit. Beep, beep, beep says the fading and ornery old computer. $28? Accepted! Beep, beep, beep. Cut and paste the address into Google Maps from our current location... which is? I dunno, just put the town we're in, quick! Beep, beep, beep!! Needs a captcha before it'll send the directions to us! Wrong?! Fuck! Type it again! Fast!! Got it right. Hit send. The computer dies. Our new smart phones receive the directions via email just in time.

After a high five and a smooch, we're back on the road to Austin. While driving, we discuss what to do for food. I pull over at an H.E.B. store in the middle of the last town for 80 miles. How much is left on the other credit card? $15. Okay, loaf of bread, chicken dogs, salsa, beer, smokes...$10.48. Phew. Made it. We're back on the road. I'm just glad smokes are so cheap here!

We have a place to stay, gas in the car, and food... for now. But still, we're not out of the woods. We're depending on the money showing up in the regular bank accounts by morning so we can pay down some credit cards and avoid any overages...and cover more of the little things like eating, buying gas, and another night at the hotel. Let's not forget that we also have cell phone bills to pay (fuck!), occasional prescriptions to fill, a monthly storage in Chicago to cover, and always there are unexpected needs. My boots having a huge hole in the sole and they're my only footwear is one. Further spinning our tiny tempest of uncertainty is that, other than one show I have booked and a scheduled photo shoot for Megan in a few days, we have no firm hold on work in Austin, as it looks like a couple things we had set up fell through... and they did. Boy, did they!

We were supposed to settle in to Austin with jobs at a local music venue. We even had a house to rent. The only money we hadn't tapped was the money we had stashed away for securing our place and starting work. Now, we come to find that this venue, a historic restaurant and bar, is behind on renovation because of its historic status. That always slows such plans. Thing is, we never heard this from the owner.

The thought of abandoning our original plans, heading back north, and regrouping from a family home in the woods of Wisconsin is not appealing to either of us. We had planned to land in Texas to stay, making Austin our base of operations. This feels like failure.

Our choice to leave Chicago was not made on a loose whim. We weighed our options there and elsewhere, made lists of what we want, like and need, compared them, researched locations... for a good six months. After traveling to various places (25 cities) during that time and eventually deciding on the Austin-area, we made meticulous plans for a 45-day tour that ended at our final destination. Along the way, we saw that even our conservative expectations were not being met. We adapted. We kept the faith. We remained confident in ourselves, and the strength of our actions. But, ah, how expectations and planning are no substitute for what life has planned! That's real clear.

We've been consistently surprised and delighted by the constant words of support from people all over the country and deeply appreciative of the money that's come in through merch sales, tips, and pay from shows, as well as online "tips" through the website. Who would've thought that people would feel compelled to send money to a couple touring around in their Little Blue Honda? It became clear that we were doing much more than that in the eyes of others. People commented that they've always wanted to do what we're doing--throw caution to the wind (even though we at least loosely planned it all out) and travel town to town on luck and a prayer like gypsies. We're reminded that music used to be shared primarily in this fashion and that before recordings, those of some financial standing would provide for the musicians in order that they could enjoy having music provided all the time. Even in more recent generations, musicians would travel in whatever manner they could, and in each town would hopefully be welcomed by the locals. If they weren't run out of town or thrown into jail as vagrants, they might be fed and given lodging in exchange for their entertainment. It's the feeling that we're not only keeping this tradition alive (minus the threat of jail), but hopefully inspiring people to take greater risks in their search for a better quality of life, that has been part of our mental and spiritual fuel in these ongoing travels. In fact, this always fuels our drive as artists. But thinking of these perceived higher motivations makes the prospect of being stopped in mid-flight that much more upsetting.

Still, we know this trip isn't over and the question of success will be judged after the effects of our work, not by the immediate situation. This is another leg of a seemingly never-ending sporadic tour. But it has been the most poignant stretch, as it marked our departure from Chicago. Where we go from here may be up in the air, but at least we'll get there. After doing this as many times as I have, I've become used to a certain scenario, much like our hunt for the cheapest hotel as the computer died.

"Cut the blue wire...no no no! The green one!" 9-8-7-6..."Wait!" (Suspenseful pause) "the red one!" 4-3-2...snip...beeeep..."self-destruct aborted."

"Well done, MacGyver."

Response From Megan When Asked About Touring

"It's kind of like when we were out in the middle of The Everglades with Phil's high school friend and his tiny boat stalled while long hungry gators swam all around us licking their chops. Really, really fucking scary... and, really, really fucking cool."

84

On The Biz
Through Non-Scientific Research Methods

Chicago Music
Then And Now, Now And Then... Zen and Tao

Let me tell you a story while the crowd gathers... it was March 4, 2004, that himself passed away quietly after battling cancer and Alzheimer's; but the years leading up to that point are what truly matter in the great histories of the world. The life of Bob Circle would require volumes to imply and whole forests to give detail. His life was that of the great generation, and the consummate raconteur. His life was that of many other men of his time but remained uniquely and deeply tied to his Appalachian heritage and the stories passed along by the words of his elders and the youngens who followed, each re-telling gaining a bit more color and length than the previous. In time, this particular aged son of a great man may put it upon himself, or be pushed by some sadistic friend or family member, to render Circ's life down on the page. Bob Circle may be resting in peace, but he will also live for many more to hear from... there is his true peace and profound legacy.

What the hell does this have to do with music? Pops loved it. He was raised on the bluegrass ramblings of Appalachia and the old Welsh and Irish classics. When he was 10 and came to Chicago for the 1933 World's Fair, he was exposed to the lively age of jazz. During World War Two, he traveled the world and was surrounded through six theaters of war by the music of his brothers in arms and the various cultures within which they found themselves. He loved Greek music, for instance, after a stint among the islands.

This is, in essence, the experience of 7 billion people. The love of music pervades the entire world. The need for music runs deep. Each musician has a vast audience, more vast than ever before. Each also has more to tap into for influences from which to sponge new ideas. How was that audience tapped into two hundred years ago? One hundred years ago? Twenty-five years ago? What do we suppose has changed?

Here's a little blog I wrote some years ago:

I'll bring you down easy like. So, you want to be an artist? You want to change the world. You have brilliant new ideas meant to inspire. I tell you to go for it. I tell you to go for it, while knowing the intense let downs you'll run into; the hell-bent-on-making money venue owners and vampiric agents you may have the occasion to deal with; the pathological pathos that seems to run rampant through our American culture; the people throughout the world that will listen with great appreciation to your work online (for free) and never buy a single download; the many mindless jobs you'll have to work to pay a pittance for rent in a shit neighborhood; the complete lack of respect and/or pitiful look you'll receive when you tell someone you're in the arts. Then, when you've latched on to this and are ready to throw in the towel and exit the ring, I'll tell you this: They need you. You chose it. Now give it your all or die with tremendous regret. See you in the ring.

Dark or true? I may have been a bit jaded when I wrote that, but not by the music "industry" as much by the constant complaining of so many of my compatriots about the "state of things" in our little worlds. And that's just what they are... little worlds. As we live in this vast world connected so closely by modern technologies, social networking, websites promoting our music with long lists of others, it's certainly easy to feel small. But look at it in another way. Two hundred and more years ago, the only way our work could be heard was by playing it live, in front of other physically present human beings. Then we'd move on to another village or city or encampment and share again.

By a hundred years ago, recording came forth with the wax cylinder followed by the phonograph, neither of which most people could afford, but it did allow for preserving any musical performance in the moment. In fact, a guy named James Petrillo was no fan of this and instigated a musicians' strike from 1942-44 that amounted to a ban on recording. There's a band shell in Chicago's Grant Park named after him now. Add radio and film to recording, and now we have most of the available forms of performed musical preservation, of potential germination for the spread of music.

By the time I was out in public performing on a regular basis and looking to music as a career, one was able to make home recordings with an affordable four-track portable studio that set your music onto cassette in an analog format. If you were industrious, you also had a cassette duplicator like the one I picked up from a friend with a studio. Then you could go to this new place called Kinko's and print out little inserts and you had your own music release. You could sell it to people on the street and at shows, or as so many did with these and then CDs, give them away. I very much discourage this latter move. Be careful not to devalue your work. Even if you have a friend who's a mechanic, you at least give him a six-pack for changing the oil on your car. Ask for something reasonable for your music. It can be as simple as a favor. I'll give you a download if you join my mailing list. At least you're exchanging something. If people truly want what you have made, they will happily share wealth and time and effort. They will recognize the value of what you have created and want to help keep it alive.

Music does not change per se. At its core, it remains a means to tell stories of love and frustration, of victory and defeat, of life's journey. It only evolves, growing new branches of expression, new means of creation and preservation. It survives. It is a living, breathing thing, and this is why we all gravitate to it. It is our most consistent symbiosis. What changes is the nature of the business surrounding it. But one has to separate the business aspect from the creative. Otherwise, you begin to hate the thing you loved, as if it's the fault of music that we've fallen prey to money. Oh, and it's not.

I've made my living in music for decades. Sometimes it's been a very comfortable one; sometimes a very sparse one. Two things got in the way of my love for it: thinking my success as an artist was based on financial gain and thinking that my so-called rock star image required I act a certain way. Both were nearly my un-doing. Coming back to the core of the creative process and playing music for pure enjoyment (for myself and others) has made it the divine selfish behavior it is meant to be. I benefit by making music, other people enjoy it and I'm therefore giving to them, they give back their appreciation, I benefit, they benefit... ad infinitum.

When I look back over the fifty years I've been around, I don't lament the change in musical ideas. I celebrate it. I'm glad that things aren't the same. How boring would that be? Being a genetic gypsy, as well as one at heart, I truly enjoy being on the road. Why? It's always new. Even if I've been there before, it's much like playing the same song over and over again through the years. Each time, it's still recreated in a fresh performance to a different line-up of audience members through a different life moment. The experience is never quite the same. What a relief.

So, as you sit there and piss and moan about the changes in the world, or act as if those old timers never had it as good you, remember one thing: The music doesn't change, we do. Without our individual growth, without cultural evolution, we don't gain new stories, new mores to work through. Without musical expression, we talk about it and our voices become flat and monotonous. It's the rhythms and the melodies that make it so three-dimensional. Now, we can preserve it through the ancient oral tradition, through the recording process; we can let it evolve and take new shape through different interpretations; we can let it live within us all and connect us all. Yeah, I know… "hippy." Too bad it's true.

How does a city like Chicago fit into this little story? First, it is part of a much bigger story. Chicago is where people like Mahalia Jackson and Muddy Waters changed the face of American music by altering peoples' tastes in it. To paraphrase someone I read about, if you take Chicago music out of American music, it wouldn't sound like American music. As just one person among millions who has grown up around the music of this city, I can see the evolution and I can see the original germ. They coexist. It has not changed since I was a child enjoying my new transistor radio, listening to the AM dial and dancing down LaSalle St. to see my Pops at The Board Of Trade Building. It still permeates every move through this great city. It continues to grow while remaining attached to the same roots. You still hear it everywhere, in all its forms, more than any city I've ever visited. And I've been to all the big ones in this country and several outside it. We have the most vibrant, living, and evolving music scene around. Be part of it. Enjoy it. Wherever you are, you can find it. The thread may change colors, but the fabric remains.

Booking

Out Of Town

It seems that if you're completely straightforward when booking a city you've never been to, they either have no use for you or will at least direct you to a venue that'll work for you. If you have something unique to offer, they may fit you into an opening spot. This is always a great start. So, find something unique. For me, it's often that I'm from Chicago. However, there are a couple cities where they have a dislike or jealousy for Chicago. I don't know why. But I've seen and heard it. Know something about the town you're hoping to play.

Booking is a tricky game. The people who book are either complete bull-shitters who want you to fill their empty space with beer drinkers because the owner never quite figured out how to do so or how to keep them coming back; or they think they're the great gatekeepers and stand, therefore, somehow above those of us that use our creative skills to bring light into folks' lives. The exceptions are there, but rare. Be advised. They have an agenda. But, so do you. It's best, then, to remain somewhere in the middle about your value. Talk yourself up, tell them all you will do to promote on your end, but also expect something from them, and make sure they know it. Don't be afraid to set a rate and remind them to get you in the listings. Ask them to use any and all media ins they have to get you a feature or at least a blurb--radio is even better. Where media are concerned, being from a big city and going to a small town only helps you get attention. If everyone does their part and the gig is a success, it will only build for the next time, as both parties are appreciative. If it's a bust, well, so be it. Maybe you snagged a few new fans in one more town and can return there to play another venue. Such is the business of the independent.

To Book Or Not To Book
At Home

One thing I'm finding more venues getting back to is going with a percentage of the ring, versus a small guarantee. Working this approach for payment can make it unnecessary to charge a cover. I, for one, will not play a venue without feeling fairly confident that I'll walk away unscathed, i.e., I rarely come out of pocket. The minute some place leaves me paying after the fact, I never go back. If a show is lightly attended, but both sides are upbeat about giving it another shot and it hasn't cost me anything (and that includes coffee and a sandwich), I'm up for it. Boundaries, however, always maintain boundaries, or you set yourself up for trouble. "I just wanna play" is not a good reason to screw yourself and every act that follows you into a venue that "just wants to make money," now is it?

Places that charge a production fee are very common. When it's a venue that you just have to play for whatever reason, you want to check on one thing. Make sure that if the production fee isn't met, you don't have to cover it. Some of them will require a check up front for production. You are now presenting your own show. This being the case, be sure you get absolutely everything out of the venue that they imply they can do. Then, be absolutely certain that you get a crowd.

With regard to a cover charge, the best sign that you're likely to be in the black is when you work directly with an owner or manager, not an agent. Contracts, as well, are not worth the paper (or PDF) they're on. The most powerful thing to remember, is that they need the artist, and if they're a bar looking to bring in beer drinkers through you, abdicate the throne. If the first seven patrons' cover goes to the bar, avoid it. It's far more reasonable for them to want a small percentage to cover a doorman and/or soundman. When they take the same risks as you, they're more likely to do their part to bring bodies in the door.

One would hope that any venue of any size would know that they need to, above all, create an appealing environment for drinkers and music lovers alike. Oddly, many seem to miss this key element. Look for the ones that understand that they provide a valuable service and have some pride in doing so. Lastly, if you host an open stage, never do it for free and make clear to the place you're in that it may take time to build up a crowd. When running an open mic, you want to always do your part to bring talent in the door. Be an amazing host who's friendly to each act that comes to play. Thank them for being a part of it all when they leave. Everyone should and can win. We'll keep our music communities lively by making them communities in every sense.

Why You Shouldn't Drive Into Trees

My Dad used to love to complain about how stupid people can be. He once pointed out an example when we were driving through Ohio to go visit his brother, my Uncle John Circle, in Columbus. Pops preferred country roads to interstates, and as we approached a small town along this one U.S. highway, arrows, reflectors and flashers directed us to the right as the lanes split around a median that was indicated by a massive black and yellow, reflector-bespeckled railing. I commented on how strange that was. My Dad went on to explain how there was an ancient oak tree on that spot for many years, and when the road was put in, the town didn't want to remove the beautiful old thing, so they paved lanes around it. It wasn't long before several people were managing to drive right into it though, so the town put up warning signs-- Don't Drive Into The Tree. This didn't do the trick, so they added reflectors... then flashing lights... then arrows. After years of moronic drivers slamming their cars into the poor misplaced tree, the town finally resigned itself to cutting the old oak down. Now everyone just slams into the median and no flora or fauna are harmed save the human idiots behind the wheel.

My Dad promptly jumped on this great new opportunity to point out stupidity and then, in his endearing old farmer-come-raconteur way, turned it into an anecdote on how change or the unexpected affects people, i.e. poorly. He was a student of Milton Friedman at University of Chicago. As a result, the effectiveness of his constant demonstrations of how no one understood economics spurred me to start (and not finish) a graduate degree in history and economics. Now, he had always wanted to write a book. So, as we drove winding country roads in Ohio, I told him he should write it on economics and call it "Why You Shouldn't Drive Into Trees." He never got around to it, as it wasn't long before the unexpected took him. But, in deference to Pops, I'm using his book title for this little blog on the music industry and the not-so-unexpected lack of initiative and creative response to its changing nature. People really can be stupid. Or at the very least, shortsighted.

In 1998, I was researching the effects of all the major record company buyouts going on in the industry and came across a speech that Courtney Love gave at the International Songwriters Salon about the standard record contract and how the bands got screwed. She demonstrated that an artist could easily end up owing the label money after a successful release. I was a little appalled, to say the least, and thus began my advocacy of the independent musician and tons more research.

Here's a typical example, from more recent research, of a major record contract and what it'll get you. That's right, nothing much has changed in the standard record industry in twenty years. Scenario: You meet in a fancy office with a suit who tells you something along the line of "have a cigar, you're gonna go far, you're gonna fly high" as he slides a check for $100,000, a contract with little pink highlights on it, and a Mont Blanc Pen under your nose. You see dollar signs and a dream coming true, and without doing much more than scanning the contract and nodding knowingly as if you do, you stick out your lower lip, raise your eyebrows, and sign. Some niceties are exchanged as you hold the check and try not to bounce excitedly like a four year-old on bathroom break. Plans are made for recording sessions and for you to meet with your A&R person (that means artist & repertoire, if you were wondering), and you head straight to your bank to bring your account balance up to $100,050.39. Now you can pay your electric bill.

As things progress, you find out that the label controls the creative process, choosing who plays in your band, what songs you play, where you record, who the producer and engineer are. Pissed at the prospect of adding Kanye to your country tune, you go to your A&R rep, throwing a fit. He calms you down with a load of propaganda about how these things work and you're in the big game now buddy, so you'll have to play by the rules... but don't forget how lucky you are! But, I'll talk to the boss (he doesn't) and I'm on your side (he's not). Now go enjoy some of that money we "gave" you.

Here's the thing about the $100,000 they "gave" you. It's recoupable, an advance on potential future profits. With the standard 2.3% you receive from net income on your CD, you won't see another check until you've sold, get ready for it, a million copies! Once you've accomplished this, your second check will be about $38,000. For the million albums of your music sold by the label, you get only $138,000. And don't forget, this puts you in a 36% tax bracket, so if you don't have some pretty clever accounting techniques, you need to hand over nearly $50,000. You end up with $88,000 when the label walked away with somewhere around $6.5 million. Oh, did I mention they also took 50% or more from your sales of T-shirts and other similar merchandise? Oh, did I mention that they gobble up a high percentage of your mechanical royalties from radio play and online streaming? Oh, did I mention that they have the ability to sell your songs for synch licensing to whomever they please without your permission? You may end up hearing your music on a pharmaceutical ad or in a movie that sucks ass. Oh, did I mention we're talking about your music? Oh, did I mention that without the artist, the record industry would be non-existent. Guess I don't have to, but this is what all-too-often happens in an artist's desperate desire to "get signed." It's not all it's cracked up to be. If you're not careful, it's far worse than being an independent scraping for money.

Time for a commercial break where I quote Hunter S. Thompson:

The music industry is a long plastic hallway lined with vampires and sycophants... and there's a bad side, too.

So, why this business practice that makes you feel you're caught in Buffy, the Musical? I've looked over the question of piracy as an excuse for the major record labels to take so much and give so little. But, as it turns out, there's a great deal more evidence that allowing fans some free downloads is a very effective way to boost sales. As an artist, I'm typically delighted to find that my music is being heard. Sure, I'd prefer everyone bought my music, but how's downloading any different from when I was a kid and my friends and I would exchange albums and then record them to cassette? It really isn't. And we still bought the albums eventually... you can't de-seed pot on a cassette case. In fact, many bands have followed the example of The Grateful Dead and actually encouraged piracy (at live shows, at least). As for how it leads to sales? Here's a personal example: While on stage at a show, a reviewer (who could've gotten all my music for free as a member of the media) walked over to my merch table and said to my wife, "I feel bad, I've downloaded most of Phil's music for free from the web, let me buy some."

When we examine the question of overall sales in the record industry in this country, we finally come to real indicators of what's going on. In the 10 years leading up to 2013, total U.S record sales across all genres, as reported by the Recording Industry Association of America (RIAA), had dropped from $14.5 billion down to $8.5 billion, or 41%! The previous 10 years, they went up about 4%. Just between 2008 and 2009, total digital and physical music sales registered with RIAA dropped 12.3%. This includes all forms of media through which music was bought... which by the way, as of

2009, included a relatively small percentage where downloads were concerned (18% of the total).

I suppose one question is whether a drop in sales justifies the kind of prices labels charge for music in the physical format, while their artists receive as little as 2.3%, or if there's another factor. The only immediate and legitimate issue that comes to mind, though, is the aesthetic aspect of the music being released by the mainstream record industry and the fact that people have more choices now than ever, thanks partly to the internet. Put another way--now this is only conjecture--most mainstream music releases contain increasing waves of blandness. But anyone who hits a local music venue or the web can find any number of independent musicians (like myself) who sell or give away downloads and offer quality CDs of great music for a low price. I, for one, keep my retail prices down because the actual cost of each piece is ridiculously low, even when you include studio expenses. When you also consider the average person's wages and the cost of living, there's no good reason to be pricing an item at 10 times more than the total costs.

As of the end of 2015, the RIAA recorded that there was an increase in record sales nationwide. It was just shy of 1%. This may indicate that more lesser-known artists are getting heard and people are starting to pay for their music. How can we tell? We can have a look at the breakdown of where the sales happened. In 2015, 2.9% of income came from synch licensing, which more often than not uses the music of unknown artists. It's cheaper for the movie and television producers. By the way, it pays very well for someone who's not making millions or even hundreds of thousands. It was also up 7% from 2014, so this bodes well for us indies. Add this to the 28.8% of sales of physical media (like CDs and vinyl), and we have only a third of the total recorded music sales reported by the RIAA! 34% of sales came from digital downloads purchased for keeps. The balance of income came from digital streaming on the likes of Spotify, Pandora, and YouTube. This is where you only get a penny per stream. That's a lot of streaming! And, streaming was up 52% from 2014! This is where I see the biggest indicator of independent music being more involved in the overall reported income from the recording industry. It's low risk for the listener to scan through unknown artists who "Sound like" someone they already enjoy. They can just add the songs to their play lists or favorites and let them pop up or look for them easily enough… and never purchase the album. One more interesting observation regarding industry sales is related to vinyl. Physical album sales were down 10% in 2015. But vinyl sales were up 32%! This put vinyl at its highest sales level since 1988! For you kids, that's when cassettes were on their way out and CDs were just a couple of years into their infancy.

2016 was a year of significant progress for the American music business. Powered by 22.6 million subscriptions, streaming overtook all other formats, generating the majority of industry revenues for the first time. Overall retail revenues grew 11.4%. These are the industry's biggest gains since 1998! Interesting additional data, courtesy of

RIAA, continues to shed light on the alarming rate of change in the way each individual can actually have a personal say in their musical choices. This runs completely against the industry's long stand in music marketing. How is this possible? Simple. The music industry only ever knew how to market. They didn't care so much what any of us wanted. Now they have to listen, one would think. It's hard to say if they are. But again, who cares? We choose now, more than ever.

63% of fans follow artists on Facebook. Americans spend 4 hours or more each day listening to music. 51.4% of revenues in 2016 were from streaming. 24.1% were from downloads and ringtones. 21.8% were from physical sales. So, why are major record labels still spending $2 million on average to break a new act into the mainstream? My answer is not so scientific. I use no knowledge of economics or industrial and organizational psychology. Disclaimer done, here it is: because they're idiots. Every trend points to how much money can be made in small bursts from lesser-known acts simply being made accessible to the world. This is great!

American consumers are spending less time responding to what mainstream media tells them they should buy. They are more often deciding for themselves what's worth their time and hard earned income. And once they find something they like, they spread the word with friends. They tell their extended world through social media.

But even independent artists like myself can find that it's a struggle to turn online or other media attention into sales. For one thing, plenty of aspiring songwriters and bands will actually give their music away at shows, in its physical album format. I very much discourage this. I've hosted many open mic nights and showcases over the years. Often times, when the bar is closing they have a whole new collection of coasters, i.e., all the free CDs that patrons were accosted with. It's one thing to offer a free download once in awhile to get your tunes out. I do this for a limited time with every new release, and with any as-yet-unlicensed recordings of cover songs. I also will offer a free download for something in return. As I mentioned previously, people want to help, they want to give you something. Once again, it's a bad idea to completely devalue your music by handing it out to everyone, especially to those who could care less, or worse, to those who were willing to pay for it. I've seen this unfortunate trend affect whether crowds at shows bought CDs from the acts they came to see. We may be seeing physical sales for independents fall to a slow dribble when we take into account the overwhelming amount of online music out there. It's tough for everyone, overwhelming, even. There is very little to help any listener decide what's worth hearing. A thousand "likes" means nothing if you can't tell what sort of music the "likers" enjoy. Everyone has their own ear. So, what do we do?

As a listener, just be picky. Don't jump on an act because they're cute, well dressed, ironic, politically edgy, or someone else told you to... don't grab the first candy off the rack. Look for music that truly intrigues you. Ignore the status quo. Be a unique listener, not a eunuch listener. You're just going to have to dig through the garbage a bit sometimes. And sure, hit those "like" buttons, share what you enjoy, and make playlists. You can and do have an effect on whose music is heard. The more specific you are, the more proud you are of your unique tastes, the more you help to pull people away from the apparently not-too-bright mainstream market.

As for we songwriting types? It seems that many people in the media are still getting all hot and bothered about all the "new" opportunities available for musicians via the internet (for the last 20 years), while we're standing around wondering how to keep our livings alive when every band has a CD and a website or five, and the internet *is* inundated with just as much crap as the mainstream. How do we approach this ever-changing business we're forced to be a part of in order to eat? I've inquired with some music-marketing gurus about this. One in particular stands out because of his success and what he's done with it, how he's turned to helping educate and inspire above all else.

Here is a portion of a response I received from Derek Sivers, the founder of CD Baby. He later sold the company to Disc Makers for $22 million and put the money into a trust for education. I emailed him asking for a short state-of-the-industry statement in preparation for this book of mine. Ya ready? Take it, Derek...

Yep, CD sales were never very clearly directly linked to online activity. One of our biggest sellers never had any online promo, but sold a ton, just from people browsing CD Baby, finding it, loving it, buying it. Sometimes our biggest

103

sellers were touring artists, sometimes online-only artists. All depends.

I agree it's hard to make a living as a musician. The music business might end up kinda like the poetry business is today. That is: There are a few who are able to be full-time poets, but nobody would get into poetry for the money.

It is still possible to make a living in this environment, but it's going to come from assuming that the old-school music industry can't help you in any way, and you're going to have to find your own entrepreneurial way to reach dozens then hundreds then thousands of people, one at a time. Do something so jaw-droppingly amazing that people who see or hear it tell all their friends and grow your audience organically. It'll take creativity, communication, and learning, but it can still happen.

Creativity, communication, and learning… sounds like three things a musical artist comes by pretty honestly. But how much do we use them? The creativity is a given with regard to songwriting, but what about creative business ideas? The communication through art is clearly there, but how often do you let people know you're out there with something worth saying? We have to constantly learn new approaches to our story telling and love songs and such, but how much do you research the constant, and I mean constant, changes in technology that affect creativity, communication and learning?

Let's go back and look squarely at some more numbers. I'm an independent who doesn't need to press thousands of copies of my CD to have a nice in-stock inventory for a while. A thousand will stick with me for a bit. Prices are such that I can easily enough get this number together in eco-wallets (no plastic jewel case and very much the standard these days) and pay 99 cents per CD. Say I spend as much as $8000 on the total production. This includes studio time with a full band, my initial 1000 CD inventory, 100 download cards, a box of stickers to last 'til the end of days, a box or three of T-shirts in a variety of sizes, and some level of advertising in whatever form.

I plan on flipping every dollar from CD sales initially. I price the album at a reasonable and mid-market retail of $10 ($12 with shipping). For easy math, I'm going to throw out the assumptive giveaways and say I sell out my entire inventory. Now I have $10,000. I've recouped my initial investment that included other merchandise. I now have $2000 in profit. I spend $1000 on my next batch. I'm left with $1000. I flip the next batch at $10 a pop. I have another $10,000. I spend a grand on more, flip 'em, buy more, flip 'em. I'll cut to the end of the story.

We don't have to do this to the tune of a million sold to make $138,000. Never mind platinum sales. We don't even need to get to aluminum, and we've made the same amount of money that a major record deal would get us. Literally 16,000 total sales of your self produced CD flipped in this fashion would get you there.

Remember, this was a demonstration in math. It's not fact but with a small number of extremely successful independent artists. Sales also break down in a far more complex fashion. There are also, without exception, multiple income streams for sales of recorded music. The point is, a living is not that far off. I make mine. Here's how.

For one thing, I love music from all directions. I love playing it. I love writing it. I love listening to it. I love talking about it. And yes, I love selling it. One has to eat. But I also love teaching it. So, my most consistent week-to-week source of income is through teaching private students and small groups. Am I saying you should start teaching? Not if you wouldn't love doing it. It wouldn't be fair to your students. My point is, pick one thing among the many and make it your regular income pipeline. Then, everything else is gravy and can be reinvested to continue to build the many ways your rent gets paid, your car gets gassed, your table gets food, and you stop sweating the money. I find that when I worry too much about money, I just end up worrying too much about money. When I step back and see I'm doing what I love and covering my basic needs, I'm happier. Then the most creative ideas happen, because they're based on getting my music heard, not turning it into a product. It's called intrinsic motivation. Make it purpose driven, and you're more likely to succeed.

You're also more likely to navigate with care by being motivated to simply create rather than earn. With this mindset, better ideas come to me. The pressure is off of me to "write another song by Tuesday," as John Lennon so aptly put it. Studies have even shown, as illustrated nicely in the book Drive by Daniel H. Pink, that people are less detail-oriented, slower in their work, and far less creative in their ideas, when motivated by money or deadlines. His book speaks to the Wikipedia world, where no one gets paid and, and in the case of the aforementioned, they've achieved the creation of the largest encyclopedia in human history. Ideally, it's all about the most inherent drive in humans: to do good, to help other people, and to create new and greater places and things. This is, again, intrinsic motivation. It works.

By being in no particular or unnecessary hurry to get everything done now, I find I'm far more effective. I have my music licensed through BMI for any trickle of mechanical royalties that come my way. I do nothing. I found a service that takes care of getting everything I release in there for me and monitors its use. I have my music available in every place and every form you can find. I found a service to take care of all the distribution and placement. I've found my songs in places I didn't even know they could stream them. I have a deal with a label to handle synch licensing for me... and that's it. It's non-exclusive, so I decide whether to agree to placement of my songs in movies or T.V., and they do all the shopping for me, and take their commission. I make it easy for people to find me, and I give them multiple options. They can listen or buy. They can listen and buy. They can grab a free download and donate a buck, or take it for free with my thanks for enjoying it. I know someone else will hear it. A download is easier to give away than a full length physical CD, and cheaper. So, there's your little free marketing tool. I do it a lot. It leads to more listeners. That's why I do this music thing: to be heard. Nobody will know you have something unique if they never get to hear you.

What it comes down to is this: There has been, is now, and always will be poorly put-together music available. There's also great music to be found. Nobody really has a solid handle on what works in the way of marketing... we just do everything we can think of (creative communication and learning), and something always bares fruit. This is true of the mainstream as well as the independent world. And things keep changing at a remarkable rate. CD Baby, for instance, has paid out over $250 million to artists over the years. When I first joined their site, my sales were consistent. But as their site has grown, I've become lost in the high numbers of their members. Random surfing is less likely to lead listeners to me. So now, rather than depending on them to bring me traffic, I use them as my store. Then I go put up the signs and inflatable apes to draw attention.

What worked even a few years ago may still be one approach, but you have to continue to seek out new ideas for promoting your music. Even should someone discover the biggest new thing in getting music to the world, it'll change. Only slightly more than a hundred years ago, recorded music was unavailable. Since then, we've gone from wax cylinders through five kinds of analog media into the digital age. Next, we'll be beaming tunes into our heads. Thing is, it's still going to change. Did I mention it's always going to change?

Should we handle change with surprise and fear?

No. We should take it in stride, but with an educated stride.

(Educate... Derived from the Greek "to open.")

With knowledge of the past and proper application of this knowledge toward the future, people may finally stop driving into trees.

Navigate well.

Other History

More Background On Felipe

My Grandfather, Herbert Phillip Wagner, was an accountant for The University of Michigan. He also had a deep love of music. While attending U of M, where he met my Grandma Lilias Julia Kendall, he often appeared on the radio singing in a quartet. The group was an interesting match up... two Germans on fiddle and voice, and two Hawaiians with ukulele, Hawaiian guitar, and voice. I have their promo photo on my studio wall. H.P. Wagner is holding the uke, although he didn't actually play. They thought he ought to hold an instrument for the photo. When my mother was born in 1928, he immersed her in music, and she and her brother, born later, also attended Michigan. She studied theater, music and English; her brother Herbert Phillip Wagner II, accounting. Yes, I was named after my Gramps. The first Phillip Wagner showed up in the U.S. in the 19th century. My Mom also spent many summers at Interlochen National Music Camp playing viola, piano, and singing in Gilbert and Sullivan operettas. She ended up founding a G&S group the year before I was born that survives even now, after her passing. The Savoy-aires were named after the Savoy Theatre in London, where Gilbert and Sullivan premiered their works. I even have facsimiles of the original programs from each premiere, inherited from my dear ole Ma.

My first memory is of her playing the piano while I sang "Battle Hymn of the Republic" with the phone sitting off its hook on top of the piano for my Grandpa to listen. I was taught to read by learning lyrics of songs. I still wonder why she was teaching me a battle hymn, but hey, what can you do when you're four?

At age seven, I took up piano and got to where I could sight-read Mozart and Beethoven. I can't now, but still have all the theory, as piano is the basis for it. At eleven, I began trumpet, but never developed any embouchure, so after making flatulent noises in band for a while, I dropped it. I begged my Mom to let me take guitar. She suggested another string instrument, unclear that guitar is string percussion... no bows are involved unless you're Jimmy Page. That effort lasted less than a month. I suck at violin. I pestered her further, and she broke down.

In my early twenties, I briefly added Appalachian dulcimer and banjo through lessons at The Old Town School of Folk Music in Chicago. I let them go by the wayside as well, feeling like I had an adequate understanding of them but wanting to focus on fewer rather than more instruments. I left dulcimer and banjo behind but stuck with ukulele, which I taught myself. I continued studying guitar and voice privately. Then one day, after securing a job teaching general music at a Catholic School by the Cabrini Green "Projects," I was walking past Columbia College Chicago on Michigan Avenue, downtown. I walked in, asked some kid at a table where I could find out about taking classes. He pointed at a line in front of me. It was registration. Two weeks later I was attending Columbia for a degree in Music Composition and

Performance. It was 1994. As I've mentioned, I also went through their fiction writing curriculum. Through insane class loads, some life equivalency credit, summer school, and lots of hard work, I graduated in 1997 with honors. I'm still assimilating the huge amount of information I collected and look back on my time there with fondness. I also use many of their teaching methods to this day, although my method continues to evolve and is always tailored to the student's needs to the best of my ability.

While there, I also worked as a tutor and teacher's aid. I was into it, but kept wishing they'd have me work later in the day. I was rarely good at at 8am, when many of the classes I worked with were scheduled. I was also hired as a production assistant for the Chicago Jazz Ensemble under the direction of jazz great William Russo. Bill was a mentor to me, if a bit of a pain in the ass. This seems to be the usual with brilliant people. Well, not all of them. While the friends and further mentors I made working with Russo may not have always been happy with *his* demands, they always seemed to enjoy the work I did for them. I had to make *his* expectations known... I guess I'm not arrogant enough to be brilliant... or is it the other way around? One night during a show for the jazz ensemble, I was encouraged by a legend in jazz, the drummer from The Ramsey Lewis trio,

"You're the best stage manager I've ever worked with."

I was, as much as possible, a sponge for what was going on around me in this fascinating world of music. I would sit in Russo's home studio in Chicago's Italian Village, his walls lined with original Ellington, Strayhorn, and Kenton manuscripts, doing his bookkeeping while he toodled around on the piano fixing arrangements for his latest compositions. In his late sixties, he was quite competent on a Mac and had everything well organized, even using Finale to orchestrate his music once he'd scratched enough ink on a page. He'd stop in the middle of something, print out a page, and hand it to me. I would be expecting to see some brilliant new musical work. It'd be a grocery list.

"Here's the card, run to Jewel, don't take too long. I'm having a dinner party tonight."

"Okay."

"Wait, do you know what endive is?"

"No, but I'm sure I can…"

"It's important to my recipe this evening, so be sure you don't mix it up. Go, I'll see you soon Paul."

"Phil."

He did that a lot. I got tired of correcting him. He did explain that he had a son or nephew or something named Paul, so I should take it as a compliment when he mixed it up. He would often tell me why I endeared myself to him. I did enjoy being thought well of by someone like Bill… or anyone else for that matter. I think I worked too hard to be liked and to prove my intelligence. Maybe I still do. It's a tricky balance between feeling like a nobody and feeling too much of a somebody. Somewhere in the middle lies a comfortable humility that couples to a healthy pride. I keep looking for it.

A Study In Guitar Attraction

I was dating. This was new to me. I lost my virginity when I was seventeen through what I think was an experiment conducted by female friends of mine who were convinced I was either gay or too stoned to get laid. I was not sure what I was doing therefore, having been awkwardly laid by a female friend who ended the episode with the words,

"I thought so."

Some time later, I quit getting high and moved to beer. Suddenly I found I had this great new source of confidence on the outside. I was still a bit unsure on the inside. So, it was safe to say that I was happy to gain the attention of a beautiful girl named Susan.

I was 18 and had just graduated high school by the skin of my teeth. I was at a house party in the west end of Wilmette, the Chicago suburb I grew up in. Susan and I got to talking and stepped outside. Somehow I found the strength to kiss her. We hit it off.

We got together regularly at my fancy little Winnetka apartment down the street from the 7-11 I was managing. I had all the '80s accouterments: a king-size water bed, a mural of the woods on the wall, my white leather suit, my bad short-in-front, long-in-back haircut, and several cases of Heineken. I'd buy beer off the back of the beer delivery truck at wholesale whenever the delivery guy showed up at the store I ran.

The thing was, I was a slow mover. And when I did move, I was clumsy. I don't think in all my years I've ever been the smooth guy. It's always been more like one of the notes I passed to my wife when we met at the Chicago Actors Studio. Yes, notes!

"Do you like Greek food?"

That was it. No wonder it took me five times of implications to get her to go out with me.

Okay, back to Susan. I must've spent a month or more trying to get into Susan's pants, but she was hesitant. We'd make out and fondle a bit, but nothing was getting me past second base. I really liked her, I found her very attractive, so I kept pushing. In the meantime…

Oops.

I got to know this woman from across the hall in my building. She was 27. She flirted with me. I responded. That's how insecure I always was. The fear of losing or simply not achieving would lead me to accept whatever approaches came my way. The problem was, I also felt that it was cool if I just

115

remained open and straightforward about it. Oh! Now I get open! I think I was confused.

Susan inquired about this neighbor. I was foolishly honest. Susan was understandably angry. I remained rather oblivious. I couldn't understand what the problem was... I was honest! Isn't that what women want?

Later that night or the next day, I sat down and wrote a poem to appease her one evening. Now, I'd been playing guitar for some years by this point, I hadn't yet considered it a career option. I still wanted to be a writer. But, I looked over this poem and thought,

"I wonder if this could be a good song."

I threw three chords together, and voila! I had a song.

I went and bought a gold necklace. I dropped it off at Susan's house. This managed to get her over to my place, where I sang her my first song. She melted. It worked! We still didn't work out in the long run. Turned out she was also dating someone else, a friend of mine. Maybe it was the necklace.

I then continued a hit and miss thing with the neighbor until I found her hooking up with another guitarist who enjoyed more musical skills and perhaps other sorts of skills, too. At least it prompted me to practice more.

I discovered, as the years went by, that any mention of my playing guitar seemed to have an aphrodisiac-like effect on women. Not that I exploited it... noooooo, not once. Several times. I'm afraid I saw more ass than a dentist's chair. If you think it made me happy or filled the void, it did not. Just check out the lyrics of this 2007 song of mine:

Lipstick and whiskey,

And a beautiful girl,

And the bare brick walls of my heart.

I'll admit that I acted proud and was without question a cad. I could blame my nerdiness in school and the fact that I didn't think I was attractive, but that'd be a copout. Fact is, I was a user and not only did damage to a lot of people, but hurt myself for it. I'm glad I figured this out in time for my wife Megan to come along or I may not have stood a chance at a healthy relationship.

I do still wonder if it's negative karma coming out when I break a string in the middle of a show. I never seem to break one while practicing. It's always right in the middle of a wicked riff or energized jam. And it's always the same string. The G-string. The universe has a clever sense of humor.

I feel confident that my lovely wife didn't marry me for my guitar playing. I'm certain she finds me handsome, intelligent, talented, funny, loving, and passionate. I could stop playing guitar tomorrow, and she'd remain with me. Actually, she probably wouldn't. She would never stand for me giving up the one gift I have. Speaking of wives, I'll state this next section with as little detail as possible, in after-the-fact respect for those in question.

Wife Number One

We were eating at some noodle place. She spoke in her Queens, New York accent,

"So, after I take the LSAT and start looking for law schools, what with you moving so quickly through your degree, what do you say we get married?"

"Sure," said I, "pass the soy sauce."

That's how it happened. She was a few years older than I, an attractive Cherokee, African, French mix from a family of good standing in New York. W.E. Dubois and other members of the Harlem Renaissance used to meet at her grandmother's house back in the day. We liked each other. She tolerated my escapades. That was it. We weren't in love. We felt the pressures of our families or society or whatever excuse you prefer, so we decided to get married. She wanted all the amenities. I provided them in a Lincoln Park apartment by the lake on the ninth floor, with a nice little sports car, and I was able to pay all our bills so she could save money for other things. Did I mention she tolerated my escapades?

Her uncle estimated that we'd last all of six months. He was wrong. Fewer than three months after a fancy black tie affair at The Chicago Athletic Club paid by her ad-executive mother, we broke up. I had a fall back, because I was an asshole. She became...

Wife Number Two

We had no intention of getting married, but I did move in with her to help with bills and for general convenience, I guess. She had three boys from her first marriage. In 1997, she became pregnant. Her fourth boy, my son, was born January 20th, 1998, and named after me. We married six months later.

I still occasionally try to understand why we were together. Ultimately, I think our dysfunctions brought us to each other. It seems as if everything we did to try and bond was a desperate attempt to show we had something real. We didn't really have much. We played music together. We drank too much. We surrounded ourselves with chaos.

I lost my strength to go on one night and downed a bottle of pills. A day or so later, she visited me in the hospital with a former student of mine. He became her third husband. As I laid there in the bed in some dark corner of a mostly empty floor, she said,

"You can't come home."

"I know," I responded.

I sat through the night pondering this and found myself relieved. That was all I had wanted... relief. I moved my stuff out and eventually found a room in Wicker Park to teach from and live in.

Her third husband eventually adopted my son, and I haven't seen the boy since. Looking back, I think I was looking for more relief. This time, it was relief from child support and the responsibilities of being a father that I may have wanted. I learned around the same time that this was what my biological father had wanted.

"Well, I sure saved a lot on child support," he said when I asked him.

At the time, I really felt I was doing the right thing and believed the boy's mother when she said I'd still see him. I regret it.

What Next?

After two divorces I was pretty much done with love. I became more of a jackass than ever. Still, I gave it a shot once more, and one more serious attempt at a relationship ended very badly. That just sealed it for me. I was convinced that I'd had my chance and failed. My mantra became "love is just an overestimation of good sex," and I believed my own bullshit.

She floated past me like Lauren Bacall...

Power From The People

The Blind Teaching The Seeing

I had this student. He was six years old, going on seven. He wanted to play guitar and be a country star. He played a ¾-size acoustic guitar. I'm often hesitant to teach guitar to someone so young. Normally, I would put him on ukulele, but he insisted and was already playing piano. So I took him on. Or did he take me on?

During one of his first lessons, we were joking around, and he began this fun, snorting laugh and asked,

"Am I snotty?"

When he got really excited, snot would fly or maybe drip. He could only feel it. You see, he was legally blind. He saw me as only a shadow. Who knows, I may be, whether of my former or future self, I don't know. I guess it's a transitional thing.

The cause of his ailment was a brain tumor behind his eyes that put pressure on his optic nerves and, thus, his impairment. Or was it?

I was six years old forty-two years previous to this story. I had health issues, too. I went to the Chicago Children's Hospital on a weekly basis for eleven shots in each arm, and my Mom often had to turn the car around from me going into anaphylactic shock. I was ridden with allergies, and all they could do back then was give you the allergens in hopes of you developing an immunity. Add to that asthma before they had inhalers, and it was delightful.

This, however, is nothing in comparison to what this incredibly spirited kid with a healthy sense of humor was dealing with. He started a lesson talk one day with:

"I had an MRI today, Phil."

"Man, I hate those," I said, "I get claustrophobic when they stick me in the torpedo tube."

He snorted and added more seriously,

"Yeah, but I just wanna get better."

Every time he told me a funny story, he leaned in and gave the final part in a stage whisper while trying not to crack up. And most of them began with,

"Ya know what? Ya know what? Um, Um, Um..."

I teased him good-naturedly about these vocal habits, telling him he could make a song if he could just add rhyme and rhythm. The next week he came back in well prepared. He and I kept expanding on it. He was delightful and inspiring.

"Ya know what? Ya know what? Um, um, um, I want some gum, I want some gum, yum, yum, yum. Uh-huh. Uh-huh."

All of this, he did with two simple chords while remaining vocally on pitch. Of course, he tried not to get snotty from laughing.

When I first began working with this boy, I wasn't really sure how to go about teaching him, what with his lack of visuals. Then I recalled how many times I've told students that their eyes will deceive them. Use your ears and the feel of your instrument. Come on, how many great guitarists do you see leaning back with their eyes closed and knocking out the best solos ever?

So, I'd work with him on what he had. And it was a lot. I recorded him a CD where I played each string, described each position, reminding him to trust his ear and his sense of touch. One week after giving him the CD, he could recite everything I said on it, even the quips I made on the recording. He felt the need to imitate my style of inflection… followed of course with further laughter. Humor in all hardship is crucial. All emotions are valuable, but I've always found humor to be top of my list.

It's June 25, 2012. My wife Megan and her Mom Gail are wringing their hands in the waiting room after my hip replacement surgery. I'm still under and lying in a bed in the recovery room. They're wondering when I'll wake up and how I'll feel. Shortly, Megan hears a couple nurses giggling across the hall. She smiles, turns to her Mom and says,

"He's awake."

I have no idea what I said on that morning. I was on morphine. But in the worst situation, I'm inclined toward humor. I read of a woman who beat cancer without standard treatments. She and her husband made a point of watching funny movies every night while cuddling on the couch. Laughter is great fuel. Haven't you noticed how in the moment of laughter, all other awareness falls away?

Sensei means "one who has been." Most people think of it as simply "teacher." I've certainly been... But, one who has been needs to look back and reflect on how he/she got there and understand that the one who is going may have new ideas, new understanding, fresh spirit. I often find inspiration in teaching. This little man offered me a challenge I hadn't yet faced. This is part of what I live for. New experiences can keep this otherwise easily bored old man from becoming jaded and tired.

I pray that this unexpected and indomitable young spirit will continue to inspire more people for years to come. Country Music Awards, watch out for this kid. Be snotty, my friend.

Harmonica Player Matteo

Meets Legendary Harmonica Player Junior Wells

It's 1994. The Phil Circle Band has just finished a show at The Clearwater Saloon on Lincoln Avenue in Chicago. It's 2am.

As I'm doing my usual socializing with the crowd, my brother Eric is talking with a woman he likes. He'd been dancing all night and making other people feel better about their dancing skills. Matteo is the harmonica player. I always found it aggravating and a little bit funny how he'd be packed up in about a minute.

"Okay, I'm ready to go."

All he had to do was shove his harps (harmonicas) into a bag while the rest of us were winding cords and carrying amps, breaking down a drum kit or keyboard set-up.

Here we are, casually putting our gear away and loading out and Matteo practically runs up to me and says,

"Felipe, we have to go right away! Junior Wells is playing The Mines tonight until 5am!"

Kingston Mines is a legendary blues club where they move you between two rooms to hear two different bands from set to set. It's typically about $15 to get in, but Matteo has their Gold Card. This will get us in. Or at least get us a discount.

Who's Junior Wells? To a harmonica player, he's like Clapton or Hendrix to a guitar player. His work can be found on many classic rock albums with the greats, but more importantly, his work is what many blues harp players look to emulate. There are a few approaches to playing blues harp.

One is the Junior Wells School. Matteo was very much of this one.

I go speak with my brother Eric, interrupting his courting. Next to the woman he's hitting on is an attractive Creole-looking woman with a voice like Fran Drescher (never got used to it). I bring up our plan for some late night music. Everybody is in.

We get the gear packed away. Matteo jumps in my car. The women and Eric go in the black Mercedes one of them drives. We all meet at Kingston Mines.

There's a line. Matteo heads straight for the ticket booth, flashes his card, waves at us, and we all get in like rock stars… we were, by our own thoughts.

As Junior Wells is playing his set, Matteo is sending Tanqeray and Tonic up to him on the stage. This goes on all night.

"Alright ladies and gentlemen, this set is over, please move over to the other stage for (whatever band it was)."

We do.

This happens every forty-five minutes.

All this time, I'm trying to get to know this lighter-than-a-paper bag black lady who's friends with my brother's potential date. She's from Queens. Like the accent didn't give it away. Seems smart. Says she's a stylist. Hair stylist? No, clothing stylist. She works at Henri Bendel on Michigan

Avenue by downtown. She pronounces it with a French inflection.

Time runs by, we move (moo?) like cattle back to the other room for another set by Junior Wells. Matteo continues to send him his signature drink… I never asked how he knew but expect any bartender could have told him.

The night eventually comes to an end. It's 5am. Matteo walks up to Junior.

"Mr. Wells, my name is Matthew. I'm a huge fan of yours and have learned a lot about playing harp from your work."

"You the boy that's been sending me them Tanqueray and Tonics all night?"

"Yessir."

Junior glances about, and waves his hand as he says,

"All y'all get the fuck out, you (pointing at Matteo), sit down."

I, along with everyone else, have to leave the bar. Matteo ends up spending the rest of the night jamming with Junior Wells.

The next day, I wait until late afternoon for Matt to call and tell me what secrets he has learned about the blues. Finally, my phone rings.

"What's up Felipe?!"

"Matt! Wow! Holy shit! What happened after we left?"

"I sat with Junior until daybreak, playing through tunes and getting tips from him. It was pretty hard to understand some of it, man," he laughs, "you can't see what someone's doing with their tongue on the harp. But it was amazing."

"So, what'd you learn, man? Tell me some secrets to playing great blues!"

"It's all about the rhythm."

(Pause)

"Matteo! Don't hold out on me now, man! Come on, what do I have to do to play great blues?"

"I'm telling you, Felipe," he continues with another laugh, "it's all about the rhythm."

(Pause)

"Dude! Why are you keeping it from me? What's up, how do I…"

"Felipe," he interrupts with a more serious tone, "really, my brother, it has everything to do with how we use rhythm, how we pull at it and play with it."

If you combine this with what Corky Siegel told me about dynamics, you have a pretty good handle on the two things that will really bring style and emotion to any song. It's all about the rhythm… and dynamics.

Phil And Ted's Excellent Adventures

I was the business manager for The Chicago Actors Studio in the old Flat Iron Building in Chicago's Wicker Park neighborhood. Ed Fogell, the owner/director of the school, had several other entertainment-related businesses, including a karaoke/DJ company. One night, he calls me and tells me he's got a bad cord and is doing a private party just down the street at a Tiki Bar… can I bring him a mic cord? It was convenient enough, as I also lived in the building and intended to be heading out anyway. I ran one down to him and enjoyed a free beer.

The next day, I received a phone call from him. The bar wanted karaoke on Sunday nights. Ed asked me if I wanted the gig. I paused, not being a huge fan of karaoke at the time, and asked him,

"Ed, are you mad at me or something?"

"No, why?"

"Well, you know I'm a professional musician."

(And clearly very special.)

"Sure, but this is an off night for you, the gear will be set up, you can walk over, the pay is good, they'll give you food and drinks."

Pause. I heard the words "give" and "drinks" in the same sentence.

"Aw fuck, alright, I'll take it."

I started the next Sunday and proceeded to make fun of people for their singing, wise crack all night, and even came up with "kamikaze karaoke," where you could put your friends up for a song without telling them. I also caught on to the idea that folks could move up on the list if they tipped me well. Also, the food was great and in true form, I took full advantage of the free drinks… mostly tequila.

The next day, I got a call from Ed.

"I heard from the manager at Rock-A-Tiki."

(Aw shit, this gig is over.)

"They loved you and want you to handle the new Elvis Night they're gonna start on Tuesday!"

Another pause. I may have glanced around with a confused look.

"Ed, you're sure you're not pissed off at me for something? And what the hell is Elvis night?!"

"You'll be running sound for an Elvis impersonator for the first half of the evening, then continuing with karaoke."

Yet another dramatic pause. Harold Pinter would be proud. Now I'm laughing the words from my mouth.

"What did I do wrong?"

"Nothing! You want the job or not. These two gigs alone will cover your rent… before tips!"

(Fuck me.)

"Sure, I'll take it. Same deal?"

"Yes."

So, on Tuesday I started this additional job at the Tiki bar. Let me describe the place for you. It was not a halfway thing. Every booth had dried palms hanging over them like a cabana roof, as did the bar. There were Tiki god bar stools, blow fish lamps hanging from the ceiling, your glasses were sculpted Tiki gods, the lighting was festive, the food and drinks were thematic, and velvet Elvis paintings hung on the walls. The memory was complete before it began. Once in awhile, you know you've met a lifelong friend and compatriot on your first meeting.

When the Tiki bar closed, I ended up with one of the Tiki god bar stools. It held court on my deck until my next move from Chicago, at which point I gave it to the man who married my wife and I. It keeps a view from his back porch to this day.

I was into the job awhile, mixing sound for Mark Hussman, who was actually a really fun '70s Elvis, and I began to enjoy it. I hadn't realized I liked Elvis so much. Mark made the music his own. I found out later that he had graduated from Northwestern University in theater, ended up

on *General Hospital*, and left for Vegas to do what he loved...
Elvis. We ended up hanging out a lot. He's even referenced in
my song "Surreal Life." It is.

At some point, I was watching the room and saw in one
of the highly flammable booths a man that looked like The
Dude from *The Big Lebowski*, only more cowboy-like. He was
sitting with friends and setting fire to a little bobble-head hula
girl. My first thought was,

"I need to meet this fucking guy."

I made sure the sound was good, waited for the song to
end, set up the next one, Mark Elvis continued, and I strolled
over to the booth of The Dude.

"Hey man, I'm Phil Circle. I love that you're burning
effigies in a flammable booth."

He laughed an infectious laugh.

"Hi, I'm Ted."

We shook hands.

"What brings you here tonight?"

"I fucking love Elvis."

"Right on. Gonna stick around for karaoke?"

"Absolutely!"

"Cool, we'll talk more later."

"Rock on."

Mark "Elvis" Hussman ended up dubbing Ted and his band of regulars "The Memphis Mafia."

Thus began a friendship between two of the crazier musicians you'll ever meet... if only for the fact that we tend to become 14-year-old troublemakers the minute we come within a mile of each other. It may be hard to understand how the both of us made it through high school, much less into careers in music. Or perhaps you understand it better than we.

And I'm pretty sure that stock prices for Jack Daniels and Jameson (if they are traded publicly, of course) go up from consumption whenever Ted and I get together... especially when I brought my wife to L.A. to visit with him. It went kinda like this...

"I have a lot of work to do this week, Phil," says Ted, "so you guys may be on your own a good amount of the time."

"Yeah, man, no problem. Thanks for the room."

Nothing was accomplished in Ted's world for the entire week, except a few gigs we joined him on and that fuck load of drinking... oh, and Ron Jeremy signed my t-shirt at The Rainbow on the Sunset Strip.

Ted's words as we all left the bar and headed for the van after meeting Jeremy:

"Yes, I have hand sanitizer in the van."

Another Phil and Ted anecdote…

I'm in D.C. at a late-night club after a show and a failed hook-up with a hot chick from the State Department. Well, not completely failed, but she has a boyfriend. The band has left me stranded and gone to our digs of the night… Ted calls.

"You out? I'm going to Nick's!"

(A Wicker Park late night bar in Chicago.)

"I'm in D.C." *at whatever club it was on Avenue P.*

"Oh, tell (whatever the bartender's name was) I said hi, she's a stripper I know. She'll hook you up on drinks!"

Phil And Ted's Not-Bogus Journey

Late night phone call from Ted, or was it a text, can't remember, I may have already been drinking.

"Hey brother, what're you doing? I'm off to Nick's."

Nick's is a late night bar that has long lines after 2am because it stays open until 4am, 5am on Saturday.

Turns out, I was available.

Turns out, I know most of the people that work there.

Turns out, there's a long line as usual.

Turns out, I can make a phone call and peer through the window as one of my friends, one of the tall guys behind the bar, sees me and promptly shows up at the door to explain to the new doorman that,

"These guys are always at the front of the line."

Ted and I walk in with a swagger as people wonder why we're so special (it's called tipping), and then he and I stand around astounded at the general stupidity of the people in the room, making snide comments and laughing.

(We're really not assholes, we're just bored.)

Ted sees some guys hitting on some drunk gals, grins his endearing grin, and says,

"This'll be fun, just follow my lead."

(Um, okay.)

I follow him in my somewhat socially awkward way, and we approach this strange human courting ritual we've been observing. Then Ted speaks as if to me:

"So, the first time I got kicked out of a New Orleans whore house, there was this woman in fishnets and… "

He lets his sentence drag off, I catch on, and it grabs the attention of the kids at the table who are less than pleased at our "random" conversation.

(You have to make people squirm a bit here and there, if only to remind them to be human.)

I chime in:

"That reminds me of when I had just got outa Cook County Jail... there were these two hookers at 26th and California... "

The guys apparently feel dissuaded. They mumble something, get up and walk away annoyed. The young women thank us for running them off. Who'd a thunk it would go this way.

(Interesting?)

Ted and I make various polite remarks that include,

"Can we get you a round?"

(Duh.)

We both go to the bar, I wave for one of our friendly bar staff friends, we get served promptly. There's this guy next to us who expresses disdain at his lack of quick service.

"I can't get them to give me the time of day."

I explain that waving a paper bill "politely" in the air will always help... not to mention tipping profusely. I gently lean behind the man as he does so and give a quiet-eyed wink and gesture as if I'm waving flies away. He gets immediately served. I lean in and say,

"Tip him well, he's your best friend."

Ted and I get to talking to this gentleman (and he really was) and recognizing his not-Chicago accent with a charming drawl, inquire as to where he's from.

"Norman, Oklahoma. I'm here for a hardware convention."

"No shit!" I say, "my Dad hitchhiked from Southeast Ohio to Norman where he started college, just before he was drafted into World War Two! He and his cousin that he was traveling with even outran a tornado!"

(All according to my Pops and therefore, true.)

So, this guy explains that he has a hotel suite downtown and a full expense account and wants to experience Chicago with "real Chicagoans."

Ted chimes in:

"Where ya staying?"

And the best reply came a-running:

"The Wyndham Grand on Wacker Drive, right there by the river. I have cable and one o' them minibars. My company pays for everything! I'd just love it if y'all knew some gals!"

A twinkle arrives with great comfort and drunken confidence in the eyes of Ted and myself. Here lies an opportunity to run this evening until breakfast and never again spend a dollar.

Ted and I invite him over to the table we just half-cleared and introduce him to the two young ladies now in need of filling some chairs and ask them if they'd like us all to join them further.

(I either don't recall any other names or don't include them out of respect.)

Dawn arrives... that's not one of the names... we're all sitting variously around the hardware man's suite overlooking the Chicago River. The two women are flanking our host from Oklahoma, Ted is pouring the last of the booze from the mini bar, I'm hanging half out the window having a smoke.

We'd spent the night watching movies and sharing life stories. Nothing untold happened. It's often more like this than what you hear about rock stardom. It's the music and the stories, however colored, that so many people want from the artistically inclined. Often, the creative mind has a more broad view of life or they'd have little to say.

As Ted and I declined a kind offer of breakfast from our gracious host and politely escorted the young ladies out for both duos to grab a cab, the helpful hardware man shook hands and shared hugs with all, saying,

"Thank y'all. This was what I had truly hoped for on coming to this great city. Ya ever come to OK, y'all feel free to look me up."

Mission accomplished.

I've always loved Chicago and love to travel.

Nothing makes it better for all involved from whichever direction, than living it beyond the tourist spectrum.

Where Are Our Heroes Now?

Since the initial writing of these adventures, our heroes, Phil and Ted, have both laid off alcohol. What, you say?! How can this be?! Well, Ted put it best when we were reflecting on this. He mentioned to someone who was curious about why he quit drinking the following:

"I got tired of Jack and coke with breakfast."

The guy responded.

"I never wanted a Jack and coke with breakfast."

Ted hit it back.

"I did. That was the problem."

In our mutual reflections on it, we're in agreement that we had a lot of great times when we were drinking. The thing is, it wasn't because we were drinking. It was because we click well together as people. By drinking in the non-stop way we did, all we accomplished was to gradually turn a human connection into a drink-driven connection. We both attend to the same lives we had. We both remain avid about interacting with people and loving the work that we do. We're both also accomplishing a great deal more than we did when we'd let the parties be the main drive in our activities.

Ted Wulfers is a great example of how one can thrive as an independent musical artist. He runs his own show and runs it well. He's put his music and money to smart work. He has received synch-licensing deals for his music to be heard in TV and film, he has a lucrative studio in Los Angeles, rents out various of the gear he has accumulated for use in studios. A guitar of his was used by Bob Dylan for a session! He sees his every move as an opportunity to bring his music to someone and has no qualms about it. His story telling is constantly a part of his everyday work and social life. As a songwriter that's his purpose, to tell stories. In each one, he shares his innate gift for entertaining people. His stage show is lively and fun. He never takes himself too seriously. He knows how lucky he is and will tell you so. He has a knack for bringing prominent industry names into the studio for any given production, and he's a very solid producer. Add his tremendous musical talent on multiple instruments (making him a popular session musician) and his natural songwriting skills, and you have a guy who was meant to do this and succeed. But, he needed one final ingredient. The one thing I've seen more than anything else... he has worked incredibly hard for it all. It wouldn't have happened any other way. Talent alone doesn't cut it. Or does it...

Lemmy

Not The Bass Player From Motorhead

He's less tragic and quite possibly more brilliant. He was born September 10, 1967, and named Lemuel Aloysius Roby by his parents. His mother was an editor for Encyclopedia Britannica and a huge fan of the blues. The pages of the books and guts of the music must have seeped through into the womb.

I referred him to a gig with Chicago-based (Brooklyn-born) blues and jazz violinist Ruby Harris. The next day, I asked Ruby how it went with Roby.

"Lem is a genius. Don't tell him I said that, it'll go to his head," he responded.

Lem. That's what everyone calls him. I call him that and much more. He and Matthew "Matteo" Steinmetz were key elements to my various band line-ups over the years. Their work justified mine by their willingness to play my songs. Their influence on my work, especially with regard to being true to my musical style, has been a thread throughout my career. Anytime I've lost sight of the importance of what we do as musicians, I could always depend on Lem quoting Frank Zappa:

Information is not knowledge.

Knowledge is not wisdom.

Wisdom is not truth.

Truth is not beauty.

Beauty is not love.

Love is not music.

Music is the best.

We knew each other before we began playing in the same group together. In addition to both of us practicing the same kind of Buddhism, his band Jack Salamander and mine shared some stages. One day, after going through another bass player, I asked him if he was available. I'd seen him play guitar, but had heard he was great on bass, too. I hired him for a run of shows at a dive bar on the far west side of Chicago in a really sketchy neighborhood. We played from 11pm until 3am every Wednesday, and half of my eight-piece band wouldn't play the gig anymore after a shooting outside. Lem took the gig even though he had to drive a bus at 7am the next morning. On his first night with us, I glanced back, and he was sitting on his bass amp. He had nodded off. Thing is, he hadn't missed a note! He's been my bass player and better musical half ever since.

I've often called him my Walter Becker. For those who don't know Steely Dan (Hey Nineteen), I'd have to come up with another iconic reference. Suffice it to say that my band(s) and albums without Lem would have suffered. His input in rehearsals, in recording studios, and his stellar musicianship have made him indispensible. He hears what will make my songs shine and does it quickly, easily, and with fluid beauty.

In addition to our musical partnerships, we've been friends who've grown closer as the years have passed. Initially, it was just that we taught at the same place and I hitched a ride with him from the train station after divorce number two. He'd introduce me to music I hadn't heard, we'd talk about books we were reading, discuss life in general, with very little shoptalk. When things were difficult for me in some way, his wry and intelligent wit would ease the tension. He has a way of using humor to diffuse the situation by pulling you away from it. Sometimes, his jokes take a day or two to fully understand, though. He refers to this phenomenon as a penny dropping into an empty well.

When I was hospitalized from a mental break down that was thought to be the result of my being bipolar, I mentioned this diagnosis. He responded matter-of-factly and with a glint in his eye,

"I just thought you suffered from deep depression under which you functioned, and then broke it by long periods of insane productivity."

When I tried to take my own life with knives to the belly during another break down, he quipped,

"I'm just glad you have bad aim."

The thing is, when he sees it's crucially important, he becomes a sage of sorts and digs deeply into the "what" and "why" of one's troubles. When my drinking was at its worst and the only way out seemed to be death or treatment, I would call him in the mornings in terrible despair. He'd ask in reference to our Buddhist practice,

"Have you chanted yet today?"

"No," I would respond.

"Call me back when you have," he'd say and hang up the phone.

He saw the profound effect a little light would have in my life and spoon-fed it to me. While I was in treatment, he called my wife to check up on her. He not only wanted to see how I was doing, but knew that she had to be suffering, too. He has proven in these moments that I was right to ask him to be a groomsman at our wedding. He shows that his interests often lie discreetly in the happiness of those around him. He'll play a gig sick because the music has to be heard. He'll stand quietly by a friend until he grows, with complete faith that he can. And that humor shakes it loose for anyone within earshot.

When I called him from a certain clinic where many famous names have previously walked the halls for treatment of the same disease, he commented.

"Now you truly are a rock star."

He used to call me PEP. It stood for "pompous, egotistical prick." When I stood in his driveway one day not long after I had quit drinking and discussed with him my defects of character, he said with all seriousness and sincerity,

144

"The simple fact that you even admit that you have character defects, when few have the courage to do so, is a fucking miracle."

If it sounds like I'm gushing over a man crush, I'm not. Ask anybody who knows Lem and the response will be somewhere along the lines of,

"I love that guy."

The Oops And Downs

Living Life From Full To Empty In One Easy Decade

The Legend Of Tequila Phil

In 2003, I did something I had always vowed I wouldn't do... a battle of the bands. The reason I broke my code on this particular occasion was that it was an international thing, and the first two shows were elimination based on audience votes. I had a good chance of moving up since I had a pretty decent following. Also, a full four out of the eight bands in the first two rounds would move on. Then it would become more difficult, with total elimination of all but one. The other thing was that it would put me in front of new crowds from other acts and get my foot in the door of some larger venues I wanted to play. Friends of mine worked at these venues. In true Chicago fashion, upon my prior request (and with some heavy tipping), they would be sure to get the managers out on the floor to see me.

At the first show, the other seven bands were all hard rock, and there I was with my acoustic guitar in hand, backed by a very eclectic-looking band. When I took the stage, some guy down in front walked up and said,

"You think you're gonna win this playing acoustic guitar?"

"Watch me," I said.

I came in first. I think it probably helped that I didn't sound as much like the other seven bands, as they all sounded like each other. Sticking out helps. My band usually does so.

The second show was at the same venue, and I survived that round without much trouble.

Round number three was at the second venue that I wanted to get into. When I showed up, the other bands were loading in, and there were two buses parked outside with people filing off of them, wearing the shirt for one of the other bands: Shotgun Elvis. After getting my band in and ready to roll, I found myself seated with the front man for this other band. We hit it off. He explained what he had done. They were from Indianapolis, and he owned a beer distributorship. He rented the buses, filled them with beer and fans from home, giving them all band T-shirts to wear, along with tickets for the show. I was impressed.

I laughed and said,

"Well shit, man. Looks like you're gonna win tonight."

"Never know, man. Either way, it's all good times."

From there, I decided not to sweat getting to the next round, as it was clear that in such a popularity contest, I wasn't going to. Remember, only one band would move on from this round. From here, the winner would go up against a few other bands for the national title. The final act standing went to Europe. You can see why else I thought it was worth the gamble.

As various friends and fans of mine filed in, several of

them started offering me drinks.

"What kinda shot do you want, Phil?"

"Tequila."

And so it began...

So there I was, waiting my turn to get up and play for round three of the Chicago Region of the Emergenza International Battle of the Bands. We were at Double Door, a big Chicago venue. If not so big on the list of places that take great care of the local bands. They gave each band member a couple drink tickets. After that we pay... $4 and more per beer, $7 and up per shot. Fortunately for Yours Truly, plenty of fans and friends were always on hand and willing to buy me a round without my asking. So, needless to say, I was getting a bit pickled before I even hit the stage. But, since I knew Shotgun Elvis was going to win, seeing as the audience was a sea of their T-shirts, I wasn't too worried. I was just looking to get up and give it my all, have some fun, check out the other bands, network; that sort of thing. It's what I called rehearsing before a crowd. I could let the band go wherever they wanted with the tunes, and I was strapping on the electric for most of my set, so I could shred away happily.

When it came our turn to play, we slid past the ropes. I was wearing my usual: jeans with cowboy boots (all shined up), a light blue button-down shirt, and a pinstripe jacket. My 6'5" bass player, Lem, was wearing his zoot suit with lime green shoes and tie, his long crazy red hair and beard draping past his shoulders like a Viking. The drummer, Inderjeet Sidhu, was in his traditional Sikh garb: all-white Indian cotton with his favorite red turban. His shit-eating grin shined between his thick, dark beard and mustache as he played. Brought in for this and occasional other gigs was a second guitarist, Barrett Tasky. He dressed like an urban cowboy, black felt hat with decorative buckle and feathers and all. We were a real sight to see, but these guys were tighter than a flea's asshole. They always gave me a lot to work with. 'Jeet would play with all by throwing in complex Indian rhythms when we least expected it. Barrett and I would enjoy some dueling guitars when he wasn't otherwise laying down complementary riffs through my songs. Lem would drive the band with his solid response to 'Jeet's drums and melodic use of his lines against my melodies. They always made me sound great.

I'd come to know the producer of the event pretty well by now. We enjoyed a couple late nights out after the last two shows and would run into each around town in between. He walked onto the stage and grabbed the microphone.

"Alright folks, here he is, a personal favorite of mine, I hope yours too... Phil Circle."

Cheers and applause. I walked up to the mic.

"Go fuck yourself... a one, two, three!!"

And we launched into our set.

After being introduced and telling the crowd to go fuck themselves… which induced laughter and cheers from the crowd, "uh-oh" laughs from Lem and Barrett, and an uncomfortable grimace from Inderjeet… one person after another began setting shots of tequila on the stage at my feet. Apparently, the word had spread as to my favorite poison.

They lined up so quickly I had to knock back two at a time between songs, while making wisecracks and raunchy comments about fellatio to the audience. They cheered my double fisting and egged me on even more.

Then Lem and Barrett snagged a few shots during the songs in a futile attempt at slowing my intake. While I sang and played up front, they'd keep playing with one hand by hammering the strings, never missing a note, lean down, reach around my legs, grab one, and shoot it to hollering from the crowd, then step back and keep wailing. Looked like fun, so I followed suit.

One song, normally six minutes long, I extended to 10. 'Jeet rolled his eyes at me while following my every mistake on his tablas. Another song where I make sexual references, the bass player stuck the neck of his bass between my legs from behind. We went to town. I guess the band went with the "if you can't beat 'em" philosophy that night.

As we neared the end of our set, I looked down with the old one-eyed squint and counted some seven or eight empty shot glasses at my feet. Another member of the crowd set two more in the line. I couldn't let them go to waste, so I knocked those suckers back. We finished our last song, and I staggered from the stage to pats on the back and compliments from fans of all the bands.

"Great show, man! You rocked!"

As we put our gear away, I asked my band how they thought it went.

"Well, you maybe shouldn't tell the audience to go fuck themselves."

"Yeah, and maybe try to avoid so many shots, you dragged us all over the map."

"But it was fun!" I retorted.

As I had expected, Shotgun Elvis, the band who brought two busloads of people from Indiana, won the night. I did, however, get offered gigs at both the venues we played for this contest, and appeared at each one several more times.

A week or two later, I was out at yet another venue checking out some friends' bands. While standing there, a guy came up to me.

"Aren't you Phil Circle?"

"Do I owe you money?"

"No," he laughed, "I'm the manager for Shotgun Elvis. Man, you were amazing at that Double Door show. I don't understand why a band as professional as yours even bothered to share the stage with all those other groups."

151

I thanked him for his kind compliment and explained my reasoning for playing the event. We chatted for a while, and he bought me a round. I promptly forgot that Inderjeet had quit after that show. He'd had enough. Apparently I hadn't. I replaced him quickly enough with Marke Lester. As another singer-songwriter-guitarist, his ear for subtlety in the songs allows him to create drum lines that do more than keep the beat. Adding Megan on back-up vocals and "Pops" Corse on keys filled out the line-up that I use to this day. I now have a group that is made up entirely of songwriters in their own right. It's also made up of people with a saintly patience. Or an eye for the interesting.

The lining up of shots in front of me, with the band stealing them while I sang and played, became part of my shtick for years to follow. It also made it unnecessary for anybody in the band to ever pay for a drink again. I'd play it up, too. Once, at another large venue, the guys who booked us told the venue to forego their usual case of PBR for the band. With us playing they'd need two. At that same show, before we hit the stage, people could see Barrett chasing me across the room while I tried not to spill the shot in my hand and get it down my gullet before he caught up with me.

These kinds of events, my work at the Tiki bar with antics along similar lines and my general summer drink of choice for many years, earned me the name "Tequila Phil." I liked whiskey, too, but Whiskey Bob Taylor had already grabbed that moniker. Bob and his first wife Denitha also bought me a flask with "Tequila Phil" engraved on it. Denitha's nickname for me, however, was "Man Whore." I no longer carry the flask or either nickname.

How To Get Health Care As An Independent Musician

Life Before The A.C.A

I became a guinea pig for a new asthma medication back when I was in college. They paid me and covered any and all health needs I had or encountered.

One night, I was waking up peeing every half hour. By morning, the pee contained fresh blood... what doctors call "gross." When asked if it was gross, I replied, "Yes."

I went to University of Chicago Hospital, where I was part of the asthma study and checked in, to get checked out.

Shortly, I was called into a room and consulted with a doctor.

He asked if it hurt.

No, it's just annoying.

Okay, we're going to use Doppler.

I'm not a thunderstorm.

No, it's a new kind of ultrasound that uses color.

Oh. I'm not pregnant.

We can use it for more than that, but if you turn out to be, we're both rich.

Uh-huh. You already are.

Well, true.

So, he proceeds to pull this hulking machine on wheels over to me, asks me to unbutton my pants and slide them down a bit, rubs something like Vaseline on my lower belly... what, no dinner and drinks first?

He turns on the screen, and the minute my lower abdominal area shows up, he leaps with joy, and says, just a minute, as he sees a fellow Medieval Barber walking by.

"Moshe! Moshe! Come here! You have to see this!"

The passing doctor ignores whatever life-saving procedure he's off to and comes in. They "ooo" and "aaah."

"Now watch this Moshe! There! There! The urethral jets are firing!" He looks at me. "Do you feel the need to urinate?"

I did. I even became excited watching my bladder on T.V. until it hit me... that's me! So, I asked what was up.

"You have a very rare condition for men. See that big spinning red thing? That's a blood clot. You have a bladder infection. Do you have a lot of sexual intercourse?"

"I'm in college and I play guitar."

He laughed, nodded as if he knew, and explained what they were going to do, still with a great deal of excitement. They were going to catheterize me. Um. I think I've heard of that...

So, I'm off to another room at University of Chicago Hospital to get catheterized in order to remove the blood clot in my bladder.

It went something like this:

I'm lying on my back on a cold table with my pants and skivvies around my ankles as a friendly doctor explains how this tube will be shoved up my urethra and into my bladder... without painkillers.

"This may be a little uncomfortable,"

He says as he grabs my pork torpedo and proceeds to shove the hose up the hose while still making conversation.

"So, you're a musician?"

"Uuugghhh, yeeeessss."

"Cool, what instrument?"

(The first one I can grab and knock you unconscious with.)

"G-g-g-guitaaaarrrrrgh!"

I'm wondering what the next step is, and then...

"Now, you'll feel the urge to urinate and it may be a little uncomfortable, but I want you to let it happen."

He was right. I did. He was wrong. It wasn't a "little uncomfortable," it, well, let's just say, I had visions of the final scene in *Braveheart*, as this fetishist said soothingly,

"Yes, that's it, keep going, you got it,"

And bloody piss poured into a barf pan.

"Okay, nice job. Now on the count of three, I want you to push."

(Am I having a baby now?)

"One, two, three... "

(Yaaaank, push, the feeling of an internal urethral skinning.)

"Here are some pills to help heal your urethra. You'll urinate orange for a few days... oh, and it may be a little uncomfortable."

Time to quote Zappa:

"Why does it hurt when I pee?"

At the time I was hoping I'd never have to again.

July 4, 2004, On A Rooftop In Palmer Square, Chicago

I was living with this crazy British musician named Ben. He was very much into Chicago music and would take small tours to England every year to show off Chicago's music explosion. We lived on the top floor of a three flat and even had access to the roof through a small hatch. You got up there by way of a ladder on the back porch on our floor. By ladder, I mean several pieces of 2x4s hastily nailed together with as few

156

nails as possible, to barely reach the top. There were always small parties on the roof, even cookouts on the tar-covered "deck." Nobody ever gave this much thought, I guess.

July 4th rolled around. It was suggested we throw a party with a band on the rooftop. All in the building agreed, and the word was spread.

After squeezing all we could through the deck hatch... a couple grills, several coolers, chairs, food, and people... we realized that getting the band equipment up there may prove difficult, if not impossible.

Ben had an idea.

"Well, mate, I have a block and tackle. We'll hook it to the telephone pole adjacent to our flat, and bring it all up from the alley."

Sounded reasonable.

He pulled his van around into the alley, and several of us worked from all levels, ground and air troops, and got to work hauling amplifiers, sound gear, and a drum kit up three floors on a thick rope, while one guy spotted from the higher wrungs of the telephone pole to make sure none of the equipment got damaged hitting the side of the building... it was brick after all.

One thing to understand about the neighborhood we were in. Palmer Square is a small stretch between two other Chicago neighborhoods known as Humboldt Park and Logan Square, and our place was two blocks from the local ward's police station. On pretty much any holiday in this area, the residents can be heard for miles around. There are barbeques, fireworks, loud music, gunfire. Did I mention gunfire? The 4th of July holds the runner-up position for fun to New Year's Eve and possibly two other holidays celebrated by a couple of the ethnic groups in the area. In other words, you're encouraged, by living there, to go a little nuts. Who's gonna notice? Certain streets are even blocked off for purposes of safety.

After all the music gear was lifted safely (and miraculously) up to the rooftop by several already somewhat buzzed musicians and early party arrivals who wanted to "chip in and help," Ben made an announcement.

"Alright mates, I stepped over to Indiana the other night and grabbed me some fireworks for the occasion, seeing as it's your big holiday and all that."

I asked him what he got.

"Oh, just some small missiles, a brick of firecrackers, and a couple o' things called bottle rockets and Roman candles."

Step aside for a minute.

How many times I would be woken up by Ben coming into the apartment at 4-5am piss drunk with some woman or two in tow, making all kinds of noise, I lost count. I'd ask who they were, he couldn't recall their names, and would roust me up to join the party, then somehow make it to his day job.

He was really a very smart man and quite talented, but a little crazy... this is coming from me, give it consideration.

The band got going. The party elevated. Ben and I joined each other "on stage," and somehow a keg was shoved through the porthole to the roof. It was shaping up to be one of the best shindigs we'd had at the building. There'd been many.

Then, as it was getting dark, you could see fireworks all around. From our vantage point on the top of the building, which was the same height as most of the others in the area, you could look in any direction and enjoy the celebration. I loved it. It's one of the things I enjoy the most about the city. People are completely uninhibited and feel right in celebrating a day, whatever it may be, and to bond with friends and family, eating, drinking, playing music, telling stories. Culture is expected, and everything that makes it is enjoyed and appreciated. Very few folks have a burr up their ass... but watch it, or ya may get a Roman candle up yours.

Wait, what? Didn't happen, but could have.

The fireworks came out. We started with the missiles. No one, myself included, gave much thought to the fact that our rooftop "deck" was made of tar and not completely level. So, while many of these skyrockets made it into the night sky, there were also ones that tipped over from the thrust of their ignition and flew at various unpredictable arcs just over the heads of the partygoers. Some ducked, some laughed and pointed or cheered with their beer-laden hands in the air. Then I heard,

159

"Mate, 'ow's this one work?"

He lit it and pointed it straight across the deck. It was a Roman candle. Balls of flame began shooting through the rooftop crowd. In a blur of laughter, screaming, whooping and hollering; with time slowing down, I watched the crowd split like the Red Sea. I laughed hysterically. The hysterical part probably hastened by the question of whether anyone would dive too far and get over the two-foot high wall around the edge of the roof. Then again, I may have had the feeling that nobody there was that athletic. It's hard to say.

I promptly explained that you shouldn't shoot them horizontally, but that only encouraged more. I became more than ever convinced that musicians are completely out of their minds. I don't know how far it would have gone, because police lights began to circle our building. I presume it was a combination of the noise and flaming balls flying from it. I looked over the ledge and saw a Sergeant (white shirt and stripes) walking aimlessly around our building trying to figure out where the mayhem was coming from. I glanced at Ben and said,

"I've got this."

I descended the "ladder" and then the front stairs and went out front to discuss our impending imprisonment.

"Hello officer. I expect you're wondering where all the noise and such is coming from."

"Dat, I am. Do ya live here?"

"Yessir, we're having a party on the rooftop."

He chuckled as he glanced up and saw faces peering down at us with some concern and then hiding.

"I was tryin' to figger out where all da noise was comin' from. It's tough with it echoing offa da buildings. Anyways, we gottacoupla complaints."

"We can shut down the band, that's not a problem."

"Oh, it's live," he half-asked with delight.

"Yeah."

He pondered for a minute, then responded.

"Do ya play?"

"Yeah, guitar, and I sing."

"No shit? I have a cover band. We do lotsa classic rock and den sum blues."

"Me too. I also write stuff."

"Man, I wish I could freakin' write. Well, listen, if we get one more complaint, we'll have to shut ya down. In the meantime, do yer best to keep da sound a bit lower, alright?"

"Sure thing Sarge."

He slowly scanned up the length of our couple, two, t'ree stories and leaned in with a questioning hand pointing upward.

"How in the fuck did ya get your gear up dere?"

"Block and tackle."

He laughed and nodded.

"Well, it ain't s'posed ta rain tonight, so, maybe leave it up dere til yer all sober enough to get it down tomorra."

"Will do. And if I see lights shining towards the roof, I know that's the cue to take the party indoors. Have a safe night officer."

"You, too! Tanks!"

We never had to end the party by order, but quieted it down and took it indoors until everyone left or found floor space.

Ben is now back in his home of Manchester, UK, and still visits Chicago on a fairly regular basis for shows and visits. His work in music has always been supplemental to his work in computers, but he's done quite well with the music. He's used his business savvy to put together tours that took Chicago bands to the UK, and the tours managed to pay for themselves. He also understands the idea of having a diverse line-up for shows. If everyone sounds too similar in style, it becomes monotonous if you know the bands well, and all the

162

more if they're new to your ear. Finding a common musical thread, in this case Chicago, and allowing for diversity is a far better way to engage any audience.

Another Weekend On The Frontlines

Life As A Wannabee Music Mogul

We're playing Cortland's Garage in Bucktown, Chicago. Our basic job description for this gig is "human jukebox." I field lots of somewhat annoying requests from drunken frat boys, trixies, or this night... laborers.

"Do you know 'All My Exes Live In Texas'?"

"Can you play some Johnny Cash?"

(I can and do, just rarely by request.)

And the inevitable...

"Freebird!"

To which I happily reply with my middle finger and "no charge" through a snide grin. I think I'm getting jaded.

Nonetheless, we typically enjoy this gig. Rojo the owner is a nice guy, even though he and I went to rival high schools. He takes care of our drinks and food, pays well, many of our friends or acquaintances from around the neighborhood drop in, and we all have a great time. Joe, who joins me on the gig because he set it up, lives immediately around the corner. We're also fairly sparkly by 9pm.

"I think Phil holds the record for how many shots of Jameson anyone has ever done in this bar," announces Rojo with a smile and maybe a warning.

"Well," I obliviously retort, "at least I'm the best at everything I do!"

Once we're done tonight, rather than our usual stroll over to Marie's Rip Tide or some other local establishment to continue the festivities, I head home. On the way, I stop at Polonia Liquors for some beer, smokes, and a can of Hormel Chili. When I arrive home, Megan is reclining on the couch watching *Gossip Girl* on the laptop. I kiss her, ask her how she's feeling (she's been sick), then head to the kitchen to throw my chili in a pot. I add minced garlic, onions, green chili, scallions, a tomato, chili powder, and oregano. I return to the living room with two bowls, chips, and beer, and we watch *Vantage Point* online before moving to *Buffy*, Season Five. Yes, *Buffy*. I don't want to hear it. It's our little mindless TV hour(s).

Saturday we actually awake before most "normal" people's lunch hour, shower, and head for Evanston so she can apply for bartending jobs at a few more places (one of which she gets), while I put posters all over the Northwestern University campus. We meet for soup and cider at Celtic Knot. One of the owners strolls by and greets us in his warm Irish brogue, commenting on how many gigs he sees I'm playing. When he finds out Megan is working at Duke Of Perth, he tells her to drop him a resume. They're starting to pick up a bit with the weather getting colder.

"Nobuhdy wants ta drenk mault wheskey in the warmer muhnts."

"Yeah, Patrick, we go for Margaritas during the summer."

"Oh aye! So do I!"

Shortly, we jump in the car and make our way to Lincoln Park, where I drop her off at work and scramble home to teach a student.

Then I'm off to Galvin's for my Saturday night show with the full band. Lem on bass, "Pops" on keys, Matteo blowing harp, and Mark diligently holding it down from behind. By the end of the second set, Morris at the bar has helped me to several double shots of Powers, and I'm pretty sure I'm going to be phoning it in like Willie Nelson for the third set.

When we're through, we get all of our gear loaded up, and Matteo approaches me.

"Hey man, why don't you let me drive you home, you've had a few."

"What about you?"

"I've only smoked a couple joints."

I agree, and twenty minutes later we're rousting Megan from the couch to party a little more, then Matteo goes to jump the Western bus, as Megan pours me into bed.

And then…

I just woke up. It's Sunday. It's 2pm. I'm sitting in my torn jeans (most of them are), no shirt (probably a bad idea, I need to do some sit-ups and there's this long scar down the middle of my belly) and the D'ior robe I bought last week at the thrift store for a pajama party I played at. I'm nursing a PBR, or I should say it's nursing me... back from my lingering hangover... and pondering how soon my stomach could manage some corned beef hash and eggs.

I have another gig tonight. Well, in this case, there's not so much playing on my part as drinking profusely (for free) and jumping up on stage every 15 minutes to poke the crowd with another,

"Hey, that was (insert name here), my good friend and an exemplary musician (whether or not he is), give him some love!"

Smatterings of applause happen, I announce whomever is next, the crowd claps unenthusiastically again, I saunter back to the bar while they play.

"Bobby, may I have another shot of Jameson, please sir?"

He'll join me with a shot of Jaeger, we'll mourn the Bears until I have to talk to other people again. Or some musician interested in getting a spot on the open stage will come over to me and ask where the list is, and I'll walk them over and hold their hand while they further inquire how long a set or how many songs they get, and where else I play. Depending on my mood, I may end up in a long soliloquy to them about the sorry state of the music business in Chicago and try to blame someone. I may still manage to give them a bunch of advice about how to get gigs and promote themselves. It'll end on a positive note... I'm hoping. I feel bad when I see the scared or dejected look on the face of some young aspiring songwriter with his head in the clouds, pondering his future Grammy speech. It's the sensitive guy in me. He's only there when I'm not thinking about my state of affairs, though. Again, it depends on my mood, which depends on how jaded I feel and how my shows went this weekend.

Tomorrow, I'm off. Well, I have a couple, two, three students, but no shows. I'll probably head over to Quenchers for the open mic and their Monday beer special, The Monday Flight: a collection of five top end beers in 6 oz. pours for $15. Normally, I just go for the $2 LaCrosse Lager. My girl Megan will be working at Duke Of Perth again, and I hate sitting around at home alone pondering what to do with my life. This is especially true when I feel like my life is slowly and inevitably unraveling and I'm not sure why. Ignorance is bliss?

So, it's settled. Tomorrow I'll teach then hit someone else's open mic. Then Tuesday, I host another one at Lilly's bar. Megan is finally feeling better after lingering swine flu or something, thanks in part to lots of healthy food, vitamins, and slippery elm lozenges. And whiskey. Or you could forego the healthy food, vitamins, and lozenges in this house.

So, another weekend comes to an unceremonious end. I'll have almost a week between shows after Tuesday, so I'll get some time to rest up, do some extra promo and such before Thanksgiving week when I'm booked heavily. Yup, life is kind of boring for me. I'm thinking of getting a real job. I wonder how I'd look in one of those blue Polo shirts with the yellow emblem and khaki pants. Never mind. I could never figure out register made after 1986. I guess I'll stick with the music.

Saints We Ain't

It was meant to be an innocent enough evening working with my longtime friend Dave. We met at a late-night bar where he worked back around 2003. We were loosely dating these two women who knew each other and met as a result. The relationships with the ladies didn't work out. The one between the two of us has. One time, Dave threw a party for my birthday at another bar where he worked at the time. I arrived early with my date for the night and made our way up to the private party room. Dave was already behind the bar ready to roll.

"Phil," he said as he slammed a bottle of 12-year-old Jameson on the bar, "we're finishing this tonight."

We did.
He started working in the music and bar industry in Chicago almost as long ago as I did. He managed to make his

money work for him in various little ventures over the years until he parleyed it into the purchase of his own place, LiveWire Lounge Chicago. He often has music seven nights a week that includes recognizable touring acts. I met Chuck Mosley from Faith No More when he played the place.

Dave and I are also both big fans of The Boondock Saints, right down to loving our pea coats and generally falling into good luck in difficult situations.

I became one of the regular hosts of his open mic night and later ran a showcase in the place. This was what brought me to the bar on this occasion. It was my second night in a row there, since I filled a regular slot the previous night for a band that cancelled. The Super Bowl was on. The Bears weren't in it, so it was more of a background activity while the music played. We cooked up Phil and Dave's Chili of Power, as we called it. It was very spicy. Other folks brought in additional food, and we all settled in for a cold winter's musical night in Chicago.

It started out slow. The weather was a bit disagreeable... it was about four degrees outside. As luck would have it, folks started ambling in as the night wore on. Before we knew it, the bar was hopping and musicians were lining up to play. The night was shaping up quite nicely for everyone concerned.

As Dave had provided all the backline (music-speak for all the gear you need, just plug in or hit the drums), we eventually were enjoying long jams with as many as 10 people on the stage at one time. I'd invite someone to join me, they'd invite another who'd bring a friend up, and so on. It was delightful. It was how music ought to be enjoyed among musicians. Nobody was competing for attention, and yet everyone was allowed room to shine. It was the proverbial front porch jam. The wee hours crept up on us, and then,

"Last call! Get the fuck out and drive safe!"

Dave locked the door behind the departing patrons with a few of us still left in the bar. We interacted for a while. Nobody was in any hurry to leave. Then, at about 4:15am, we heard the beeping of a truck backing up and could see the reflection of flashing yellow lights in front of the bar. Dave leaped from his stool and ran to the little window dodging his head around to see past the neon sign. He spun around and frantically spouted out,

"Fuck, anyone parked in front? It's the snow law! They tow you after 3am anywhere on Milwaukee Ave!"

"My van is out there! Shit, my van!" said one of the guys with distress in his eyes.

Dave unlocked the front door and bolted at the tow truck. The driver was in the front seat with his window halfway down. The van was part way off the ground and the driver's hand was on the lever to get it all the way up.

Now a couple things to understand: this is *way* north of where the tow trucks wait with bated breath at 3am and yank a hundred cars from Wicker Park and Bucktown; they're all

170

independent contractors, and if they've made it this far, they've made their money for the night. This, and the police have to ticket the car first, and no such thing had happened. Okay so that's more than a couple things.

So Dave, who's not a large guy, found himself hanging on the side window of the tow truck with a rather large guy in the seat staring in his face. He started yelling at the guy,

"Drop the fucking van! Drop the fucking van!"

The driver decided it would be a good idea to start rolling up the window and put the truck in drive. It started edging forward. Dave responded,

"You fucking roll up this window any further or break my fingers or drag me down the street, and I'm suing the living shit out you cocksucker!"

The tow truck stopped and was ground into park. The window slowly went down.

By this time three more of us were out on the street not quite sure what to do other than marvel at Dave's brave craziness. I shrugged and pulled out a wad of cash in front of the tow truck driver. He saw it and said,

"I ain't taking no payoff!"

He then reluctantly dropped the van. I was glad to have saved the money. Our friend's van was saved from the auto pound but took a little damage to the bumper, to which he responded,

"I'm more worried about how pissed my wife is gonna be when I arrive home this late."

He proceeded to head out. Dave and I and the bartender went back in, and the next thing we knew, the sun was coming up. Crap. I had a recording session that afternoon. We crashed at the upstairs dormitory provided for touring bands.

I woke up at 4:30pm. I had 30 minutes to get to my session. I was a bit hung over. Dave was still asleep and was my ride. I woke him, and we quickly cleaned up the bar from the previous night. I asked him for a drink to ease my pain. He blinked and said,

"Man, sometimes ya just have to let yourself be hung over," but he relented.

He then drove me to my session. I can't recall what I recorded that day or if I even kept it.

Dave walked over to me not long after I'd quit with my rough habits. I was packing up my gear after having just played on his stage. He smiled softly and sincerely with his hand on my back and said,

"Man, I think I've probably seen you perform a hundred times, and you've always been great. But tonight... you just sound more... crisp, I think is the word I'm looking

for. You look healthy and you seem more relaxed. What can I say brother? I'm just really glad you quit drinking. It's working for ya. And you're a cheaper date, now. Let me buy you a coke."

It's The Irish In Me

Megan and I were coming back from our previous night's gig in Springfield, Missouri, after a 10-day tour through Kentucky, Tennessee, Arkansas, and Texas. We were nearing Chicago. She had to be at work at Tommy Nevin's Pub that evening. They especially needed her, as it was March 17th, St. Patrick's Day. Fortunately, she was driving. I tend to talk a lot while driving and slow down as I make points. I almost always have either a point to make or something to point at when I'm driving. It passes the time, I guess.

"Ya see that, hun? Those are soybeans. They like to plant them on land with a slight roll to it for better drainage after the rains… "

"Sweetheart, you can drive the speed limit," she'll sigh, "you're like an old lady."

It's true. It's also true that she's the exact opposite. It's downright terrifying sometimes.

Anyway. We always tweet and such as we make progress on the road. It's a promotional thing. So, as we reached Joliet, Illinois, I grabbed my phone and tweeted that we were an hour out of Chicago, traffic willing. What I didn't know was that her Dad, Bill, whom I just call Pops, followed my tweets. Moments after I tweeted, my phone rang.

"Hey buddy!"

"Hey Pops!"

Megan and I were still only engaged, but had felt married (in the best of ways) for a long time by now. Therefore I treated him already as my father-in-law... in the best of ways.

"So, you guys are gonna be in town soon?"

"Looks that way. Megan's driving like Speed Racer's twin sister. She has to be at work pretty soon, so she's just dropping me and the guitars off at the apartment and then making a bee line for Nevin's."

"What're you doing?"

(I paused until I realized that he didn't know it was obvious.)

"Drinking. It's St. Paddy's Day."

"I'll meet you at your place with beer and a bottle of Jameson. We'll celebrate your people."

(He's not Irish, but nobody's perfect.)

"Great, saves me spending money at some bar full of fakers!"

He gave an endearing laugh.

"See ya soon bud."

We arrived in the expected record time. Megan pulled up in front of our place. While she ran up to quickly clean up and change, I wrangled the guitars and managed a couple bags into the apartment. Then she drove like a Leprechaun on crack to her job. Though she's not short and bearded. Or a mythical creature. Or on crack. She drove fast.

Her Dad showed up shortly, armed as promised.

I'll tell ya what. You'd be hard put to find a more pleasing deal for your father-in-law. He and I play music together. He's my keyboardist, as I've mentioned. We get along well, even when we discuss politics and religion, neither of which we agree on. He could have written this sort of book himself. He toured for many years as a professional musician. That's how he met Megan's Mom Gail, whom I also think quite highly of.

Moving forward…

Megan arrived home at 2am. Her Dad and I had nearly wiped out a bottle of Jameson and a fair amount of beer. I'd already been to the liquor store around the corner for re-supply. I wanted my wife-to-be to enjoy some drinks after eight hours of driving and as many working at an Irish Pub on St. Patrick's Day. That was my excuse, and I was sticking to it.

She walked in and heard two drunk old men singing…

"Her eyes they shown like the diamonds, you'd think she was queen of the land. Her hair hung over her shoulder, tied up in a black velvet band!"

I was teaching "Pops" Corse Irish drinking songs. Megan laughed and joined in. I forgave them both for not being Irish. We truly were family now. Although, I believe that may have been the last night that either of them tried to keep up with me. In fact, I rarely see either of them pick up a drink these days.

Ch... Ch... Ch... Ch... Changes

Side Effects May Include...

Cognates Among Us

It goes something like this...

It's not all that hard if you give it some thought, Phil. Really, it isn't. You need balance, don't you?

Well, yes, I may never attain this much-coveted thing, as most "sane" people seem to lack it.

Let's start there. You have brains and talent, in many of the same areas as individuals who are not perplexed with some negative diagnosis of the brain.

And then I go fuck it all up with over-thinking and obsessing... oh, sorry for the redundancy, but facts are facts... even as I obsess on proper grammar in the midst of a breakdown.

Find that middle ground. Start with realizing how much you do to look after people. Try that. Get out of yourself and reach out. You're not alone.

Every time I try to help, each time I've reached out or opened up, I've been screwed. Why bother. Besides, what do you know? You're not me. You can't possibly understand what I'm going through. Leave me alone.

Then, if I'm lucky, if I breathe for a moment or meditate on things, something somebody said will occur to me. Like when I was worried about making money and thereby showing people how special I was and a Buddhist mentor of mine said,

"Phil, it doesn't matter whether you have monetary success in life. You can't eat money, you can't feel money, you can't express money. I assure you, you have, are, and will always continue to benefit people's lives through your art and compassion. It's all about creating value, not creating a bank balance."

Then it continues...

Now you're on the right track.

What if I derail?

Keep your eyes forward, have faith in yourself.

I can't be trusted.

Reach out, let go and trust who you truly are. You have to extend trust to receive trust. This is especially true of oneself. Take a risk in trusting yourself.

Cognitive therapy is the creative process. The arts are the original therapy. I believe they remain the most effective.

I've survived a life of physical health issues, only to be diagnosed bipolar and addictive. My approach to surviving this has been by writing about it, expressing it, sorting it through, seeing it to its many possible final conclusions, and ultimately, sharing my experiences with other people, in hopes of helping them.

I try to sort out the things that have sent me spinning from mental vertigo, and understand the triggers. I may be a little out of my mind, or more accurately, too much in it.

When I have very little money, for instance, I seem to like obsessing on it. Obsessing on the negative only achieves more of it. "I have no money," I say in complaint. "Have no money" the universe hears. Og Mendino, Napoleon Hill, and Clement Stone were all pretty spot on, if a bit too salesman-like for our sensitive creative ears. Still, that whole positive mental attitude, magic of thinking big, conceive, believe, achieve deal, it all makes perfect sense.

Where's the middle road?

Is there a middle road?

Somewhere between the left and right, manic and depressive, up and down, inside and out, and all other extremes, lies that middle ground. The mind, the emotions, the spirit, can sometimes feel like a car without decent suspension driving too fast on a dirt road. If there aren't any cliffs or rivers alongside us, we'll probably get where we're going all in one piece, if a bit jostled. And who's to say we didn't need a little knocking about? Who's to say it wasn't the only way to get where we needed? Our choices may not always be our own, but our reactions can be.

All I did one day to be reminded of these things was take a walk down past a couple fallow fields on a country highway and let my mind wander. One hour later, I had meditated on everything I was immediately concerned with, talked to myself as I would speak to another asking my advice, stepped back and let it germinate out there somewhere in my part of the universe.

By the time I had arrived home, I had all the answers I needed at that time, and I was reminded of a most important thing: My work in the arts has maintained me all along, not just through a need to express, but through the need to give. Artists give people the expression they're looking for, while giving themselves the much-needed therapy they use to survive themselves. These needs link us all. When we deny our intrinsic motivations as an interdependent species, we suffer. That is, when we stop reaching out to support or help each other, we die.

When Cognitive Therapy Didn't Work

I was having a good day. I spent the afternoon hanging out at a friend's house for a barbeque, some yard games, a little music, and basic relaxation. I needed it. I only had eight beers. I counted. My girlfriend and I were on the rocks and I had no idea why. I had given the heart one more shot and failed. Still, I was having a good day.

When I got home, she and I fought about something. I have no idea what it was. I don't remember much. It became a blur, a fragmented nightmare. It was a complete breakdown the likes of which I have never experienced, before or since. What I do recall, I wish I didn't. It comes in horrible painful blasts when I run through it. Like this:

As we argue, I peer down at her and am greeted with a look of absolute hatred. There's a flash of anger and then I see my hands around her little throat. I pull myself away, disgusted and horrified by and with myself. I know now that I am completely lost. I am forever beyond reality. Falling facedown on the bed, I begin crying,

"What's happening to me?!"

Then there's another flash of darkness, a blackout of sorts. Now I'm in the kitchen. I'm looking down at my side, and protruding from my left gut is the broken blade of a knife. In my hand is the bloody handle that was attached to it. I drop it and reach with my fingertips for the shattered piece in my side. It slides out. I drop it. I feel no pain. I glance up to see her standing in the adjacent room crying. I think there's a phone in her hand.

"I've come this far," I think, "may as well finish it."

I grab another knife from the blade holder and walk out the back door. I lean against the neighbor's house and brace myself. My right hand counts three thrusts of aim and plunges into my side just below my ribs. I feel this one. I yank it out. It hurts this time. I realize I felt nothing of the first blade. I'm getting hazy.

"There's more blood in the movies," I think to myself, or maybe say aloud.

Black.

I wake up. I'm face down on the kitchen floor.

"Shit," I think, "I'm still alive."

I reach for the tabletop above me to see if the blade is there. A hand slaps me in the back of the head. I roll onto my back to see cops and paramedics everywhere. I stand up, ignore the gurney they offer, and walk to the ambulance. In it, I cry to the medic.

"Help me, please. I don't know what's happening."

"I've got you, man. I've got you."

I heard this voice years later as I crawled from the mud of my life once more. It's become my subconscious' mantra in tough times. I've got you, man.

Abdominal surgery confirmed I had come millimeters short of piercing my liver. According to the doctor, this would have poisoned my blood and killed me in 10 minutes. 10 became a theme. 10 days later they transferred me to the state mental hospital. 10 days after that, I left to stay with friends. I got back to work and eventually gave love another chance. It took some years before I'd ever give myself another chance. 10 years later, I figured out part of my problem.

You Were Such A Sweet Kid. What Happened?

Age nine, a little blonde, blue-eyed kid from Wilmette gets off the "L" at Van Buren with his transistor radio, ear phone plugged in his left ear... the one that later lost 30% of its ability to hear as result of a Q-tip accident. He's grooving to AM Radio, and as he rounds the end of the stairs leaving the

182

train station, a tune he's been waiting and hoping on comes into the rotation.

"Mama, just killed a man, put a gun against his head, pulled my trigger now he's dead."

He decides to walk more slowly and lets the music become his personal soundtrack, treading happily around in front of The Chicago Board of Trade Building where his dad works. Somewhat oblivious to the dangers of the city, but following all his father's directions as to how to carry yourself and who not to talk to, he waits out the final refrains of Queen's "Bohemian Rhapsody" and then saunters into the great front doors of what, in ages past (the 1940s), was the tallest building in the Midwest. He thinks of The Peoria Pig Report as he walks to the elevators. Well, that's what he calls it... whatever that thing is comes on at dawn on WGN where they ramble on about pig futures and corn and such. As far as he can figure, this is the stuff that his dad the economist regurgitates at the dinner table. Not the pigs and corn, the information.

The elevators are all marked for different sections of floors, so if you would rather get to the 40th more quickly, you can. Express, they call it. Instead, Little Phil takes the long way up, the scenic route, as his dad always calls it. This way, he can watch all the interesting, if uptight people on the trip to the top. But best of all is when the doors open, just a few floors up, to show a scene of what looks to be complete and utter chaos! Men are running around screaming at each other in these bright vests with funny ID tags that have one name followed by some numbers and letters or something. It's too hard for him to focus on unimportant details, it's all the noise and excitement that attracts him! Wide-eyed and smiling, then biting his lip, then giggling at how funny they act, he's always a bit let down when the two floors of traders have passed.

At the 38th floor, the wide-eyed one exits the elevator, turns left, and walks to end of the hall. He gets to a door that leads into a small grouping of offices with the moniker,

T. Robert Circle Economist

He walks in without hesitation, such a thing not yet occurring to him.

"Hi Mr. Bowles!"

"Hi Phillip! How are ya kid?"

"I'mokaywhere'smydad? "

(Bowles chuckles.)

"He's just finishing up with a client."

Phil bites his lip, then says,

"Ok, um, um, tell him I'll be in my office, ok?"

Phillip spins around with great purpose and walks through a door into a file room with one window wedged behind and between several file cabinets. On the frosted glass in the center of the door is another name and title. In the gold

184

paint you would use for plastic models or lead figurines, somewhat sloppily spelling out is:

Phil Circle Auther

It's not that Phil's a poor speller, he's won spelling bees. It's his unwillingness to look it up in a dictionary, there's far too much to do and his work is very important. Upon finding he's wrong, he'll defend himself easily enough. The rules of the English language are unclear and inconsistent.

In the valley between the walls of file cabinets and boxes of office supplies is a small desk with a fake wood-veneer top. This is where he sits down and pulls out a legal-sized yellow note pad and pen out of the right upper drawer and begins writing.

If you ask him, he'll tell you that he has 17 books already written, mostly about dinosaurs as monsters who've come back to life, and well, yeah, there are lots of illustrations. The pictures actually take up more than half the pages. And they're on construction paper of various colors. Now, however, he's digging into a "more serious" book about monsters, with a pile of written pages already done, and he's waiting on the pictures this time. Someone, probably an older brother, said that real books should never have too many pictures.

Losing track of time as he immerses himself in frenetic writing, he barely realizes it when his dad enters.

"Are you enjoying your day off from school son?"

"Yep," he throws out, still trying to get his thoughts

185

and ideas onto the page.

Bob Circle pulls a $20 bill from his worn black leather wallet and throws it on the desk in front of Phillip. This catches the boy's attention.

"Here ya go. Don't say I never did anything for you," he chuckles. "Go to one of the museums, and I'll meet you at Greek Islands for lunch. Be there at 12:30?"

"OkayDadthanks!"

His Dad leaves the file room, quietly closing the door behind him and smiling proudly. Here's a kid who, oblivious or not, doesn't have the capacity to be afraid of finding his way around downtown Chicago at age nine; who will delve into anything that fascinates him with a tremendous energy. He only does well in school on things that interest him, or perhaps appropriately, when they interest him.

In fourth grade, he was a month behind on his math homework but became suddenly inspired one day. He grabbed his math worksheets, hid behind the couch, and knocked out all the overdue work. He may have gotten a score as low as 90% on one of the pages, but his Dad saw only a driven boy who knew what mattered to him and seemed seldom to forget this quality in his youngest, adopted, son. And his son would never fail to recall the feeling of pride he felt from his Dad.

"Atta boy, Tiger," was his favorite phrase.

Eleven Years Later

I had an interview with a financial firm for a job as a commodities broker. I knew nothing about this sort of work except that I seemed to have skills that allowed me to sell water to a drowning man. At least this is what I heard so often from various people like my Dad.

As I sat in the interview (1986, age twenty), the potential boss ran down all that would be involved in my job, how I'd work very hard under high levels of stress but make tons of money while possibly risking becoming a coke-addicted asshole by age 35. 35? Shit, that's a long way off, I'm thinking, maybe I can just have a mild habit, be a bit of a jerk, and retire at 29? I listened loosely for questions I should think about before answering.

Toward the end of the interview, he asked,

"How much income would you like to make annually?"

I thought about it for about three seconds.

"$50,000 a year."

In 1986, this was a comfortable living. It's $110,444.65 in 2017 money.

He leaned back in his chair and let out a disappointed sigh, then said through his feelings of having been let down,

"That'd put you in the bottom 3% of our brokers."

I think about three seconds ticked.

"Well then, what's the top 3% make?

He sat back up more quickly than he had previously retreated. He smiled approvingly.

"Listen kid, here's the way it works. We don't call you. You call us. You have 72 hours to make a decision as to whether you want this job. Here's my card. I have your information. If we don't hear from you we assume you're not interested."

I took his card, stood up, thanked him, and left. I was probably a bit puffed up from knowing I could impress a fat cat behind a fancy oak desk.

The next day, I was sitting with my Dad at home talking about things, as we frequently did. It would be anything from current affairs or history to how my life was going or a free lecture on economics. We were sitting in his bedroom. He was sitting in one of his few recliners placed about the house. I was teetered on the edge of the nicely made bed. The phone rang on the bedside table. I picked it up,

"Circle residence."

It was the guy from the commodities firm.

"Hey Phil, I just wanted to follow up on our discussion yesterday. So, are ya ready to work for us?"

"Um, I thought you weren't going to call me, I was supposed to call you."

"Yes, but... you're just the kind of guy we're looking for... young, driven, smart."

Well, it's true. I was young.

I probably bobbed my head side to side and sighed before breaking it to him.

"Nah, I've decided that I want to go into music, be a guitarist, maybe sing too, write some tunes... but hey, thanks for the offer."

I was waiting at this point for the explosive laughter and a line about how stupid I am. There was a long pause and a definite tension... the pause on the other end of the line, the tension in the room I was sitting in. I tried not to look at my Dad.

"Well. Phil," said commodities guy, "I'll tell you what, you're just the kind of guy who could make it in music. Best of luck to you, and I look forward to seeing you out there."

We gave our goodbyes and thank yous. We hung up. Not such a bad break up after all. But then there was this long silence while I imagined my Dad was trying to figure out what to say. This is where the obligatory and moderately frightening sigh came in, followed by...

"Tiger, did you just turn down that job as a broker?"

"Yes?"

(Notice the question mark of fear?)

Sigh number two, longer and more breathy, with a hint of groan...

"You know something son? One in 10,000 makes it in the music business!"

I didn't respond well.

"Well then,"

said I with quite the ornery tone of voice,

"I dunno what the other 9,999 are gonna do, but this is my fucking choice! If you don't support what I do, well... well, shit... don't ever offer me another word of advice, or, aahh... a fucking dollar when I need it, or any other kind of help goddammit!"

I stormed out of his room, like the punk that I was, and went down to the family room where I was residing while between apartments. I'd been there for three months. That's a long space between. I grabbed my guitar and for some reason started playing with song ideas. Within an hour or so, I'd written a tune that was strangely enough not full of angst. It was about the intuition I always had when things were going well; that the other shoe was going to drop. Hmmm.

Once I was done running it through enough times to be confident I'd recall all the changes and such, I set down my guitar and sat back on the hide-a-bed. I turned on the TV, looking for a distraction. Now, this old farmhouse-become-suburban home didn't exactly possess the best soundproofing. You could hear fairly well, if not with great diction, through all the ductwork. I guess my Pops had picked up on the music and from the repetition had guessed I was working on something new. Shortly, a sheepish (and therefore highly out of character for my Dad) knock came on the door. I responded.

"Whadya ya want?!"

"Um, Tiger, can I come in?"

I think I grunted more than anything, but he got the idea it was safe and entered anyway. I sat moping and staring angrily at the television, probably watching *Cheers* or some other show I enjoyed at the time. (It was still a running show, but was also in syndication by this point.)

"That song I just heard you playing all this time, did you write that?" he asked.

"Mmhhm."

I watched out of the corner of my eye, trying not to let on that I cared. He nodded and smiled.

"Tiger, that was the most beautiful thing I've ever heard. You're absolutely right, music is what you should do."

I hope I thanked him, I think I did. But he never had a negative word to say to me about being a musician ever again. I heard a lot of "atta boy, Tiger" from him over the years. Until the day he died, he offered nothing but support... when he recalled who I was, that is. Towards the last couple years of his life, he only recognized me as someone he should know.

One thing Bob Circle did well was stick to it. Once he knew I was passionate about music, he never cared for me to do anything else. As far as I could tell and from what I heard him share with me, he felt the same about my siblings. He didn't always understand our choices or motivations, but he spoke with pride about all of us and sincerely wanted us to succeed in our chosen careers. Again, as far as I could tell and from what he said to me, which was a lot.

There were times I felt as if I was the father towards his retirement years. He would confide in me his troubles and even his feelings about his older brother John. His last visit to see his brother was on a road trip I took with him through rural Ohio on the country roads, just the way he always preferred to travel. He talked about his brother and their father and how cruel he felt they were to him. He admitted he felt like he was less of a success than his brother John, and that John looked down on him. I found out otherwise on that trip. Uncle John asked me why "Bobby" seemed so depressed. I told him what I thought. He went on say how much he always admired his younger brother. He talked about how smart he was.

"Why, Bobby could recite the statistics of 500 working ball players by memory!"

I told my Dad on the way home, but I think he was never able to grow past certain things that dogged him from an early age. By this point, he may have also been noticing, as I was, that his memory was going. The rest of our trip was dedicated to discussions of distraction. That's when I learned about why you shouldn't drive into trees.

Some Time In The Next Century

He's past 40. People tend to think he's younger if they don't know any better. They see him looking older after one of his long weekends playing payless shows to small crowds and wearing himself out trying to glean a living from what he sees now to be a hopeless scene. If he keeps this up, it won't be long before he looks 15 years older. Many find him a complexity... crazy, knowledgeable, wise beyond his years... depends on the moment. He is, after all, an actor on the side.

His insatiable drive has given way to jadedness. His positive words have morphed into negative fables. His face, once aimed forward and high, has become a weary eye with a vision only of the ground. Depression and anxiety have become his rulers. From days spent working tirelessly, he has moved to days spent drinking, ignoring the obvious, trying to gain back lost sleep, not answering calls, and feeling at a constant complete loss for answers.

As reality sets in through various small adventures

away from Chicago, this jaded old artist stands back, and with a tired smile and knowing nod, gives a mental "a-ha." 10 years ago, he made five times what he does now and possessed half the skills and recognition. Five years ago, he could hardly visit an open mic or someone else's show, and in many cases, any bar, without someone knowing him. He was given respect, asked for advice, greeted cheerfully. His students admired him... many going on to their own success and crediting him... other musicians knew him well and spoke about his commitment to the Chicago music scene with approval.

Then, while he found his students still thought highly of him, many folks saw him as a bit nuts, even kind of flakey. Venues had come to still appreciate his work, but always questioned his draw and even his quality of performance. And yet, there he was, more skilled than ever in his art... but to what end? Crowds dwindled, the economy decimated his roster of students, and he was spending his days in self-pity, which led to outright anger. All means had come into question when considering the ends.

But, a series of short-run small tours to towns outside Chicago began a change. People that didn't know him from Adam ran to his shows, bought merchandise, asked for autographs. Places he had yet to get to now played his music on their radio stations, both on the airwaves and online. Even still, the economics of it were troubling. Accounting for time and energy, cash spent, quality of the product, etc., shed yet another dark light on things. With all the attention, augmented by nothing but positive reviews... where was the money?

Did he get into this for the money? A quick anecdote that he shares in lessons will answer that:

"Plenty of people get into work because they're good at it, even if they hate it. Nobody gets into music for any reason other than for a love of it. Hell, who makes a hobby of accounting?"

But a person needs to eat, and basic economic theory implies that the commodity having become more valuable, it should cost more, right? Or not? Well, this is unfortunately, correct. The commodity called music has, in Chicago and the world, become so widely available it's as if a working musician were trying to convince people that the price of air should go up. You can practically fart into a microphone and someone will happily download it. And yet, do devotees of religious movements get paid to make pilgrimages? Why then should a musician, no matter his level of skill, reputation, or respect, demand more value in one town or another? The answer is no, or maybe, or yes, why not, who cares, what are you asking, I just don't know. How do you define value? What to do?

The answer is leave. Keep moving. Keep spreading your gospel. Be the gypsy that you know you are. This does not rule out Chicago as a great music town, excepting the fact that the general population is aware that there is free or cheap live music seven nights a week, usually within walking distance of one's home. For a new musical act, or any aspiring young musician, there may be no place more suitable to cutting your teeth. You'll find a scene where the competition tends to be between the artists and venues, not the artists themselves.

You'll find a place where community is the primary quality. You'll rub elbows with legends, ready and willing to share their experiences of success and their struggles. You'll hear this as much as anything,

"Hey man, great set, ya wanna do a show together?"

"Say, I really like your material, have you played (insert venue here), they'd really dig you."

"We're all in this together."

In fact, Chicago-based acts that present themselves as competitive and/or demonstrative, or put themselves forth as better than others, or give open and loud complaints about another band or musician, are considered arrogant and self-serving. They are then often shunned by the scene, if unintentionally. It isn't out of insecurity, but for the general unspoken consensus that "we ARE all in this together."

So, why did I leave again?

I never really did leave. Chicago is my home and heart, musically, and as a man and a boy. It was simply time for a vacation. But, I did try and escape. But I couldn't. I got married while I was away, but did the ceremony back home.

One Step Forward (Ten Steps Back)

Megan and I got married on August 14, 2011. We chose the date at a show the night before Thanksgiving in Madison, Wisconsin. Many of her family and friends were there. I was behind the microphone getting ready to play another set. We were getting lots of push to choose a date for our wedding. Everyone knew we loved each other and were living together and planned on getting married, so it was ripe for doing. Wisconsin has this game you play at bars with dice and a cup. You usually play for free drinks or cold hard cash. I had another idea. I directed my glance toward the bar owner on the other side of the counter from Megan.

"Do you guys have shake-a-day?"

"Of course," answered the owner with obvious in her voice.

"Hun," I said grinning at Megan, "Why don't we just roll dice to choose the date for our wedding?"

Before she could shoot me dead with her stare, the entire place went up in cheers and applause and nudging words. The owner and Megan did the math as to how to come up with the right number of months and days with dice, and the proverbial drums rolled. So did the dice.

"Eight!"

Hoots and hollers and anticipation.

"Fourteen!"

197

Great amounts of noise were interspersed with her Uncle Chris hollering,

"That's a Sunday, we're open!"

As the noise leveled out a bit and I breathed a sigh of the relief that it wasn't next month or something, Megan's voice pierced the mumblings with a whimsical hint of "fucker" in it.

"Don't I get to roll for the year?"

We had our wedding out doors on a beautiful summer day with a hint of morning sprinkles that cooled things off perfectly. When Megan walked from the car to the processional, the clouds literally broke and rays of sun fell across the meadow in Busse Woods where our families and friends stood waiting. It was a wonderful day. The owner of CAUDOG Records and Chicago Acoustic Underground, Michael Teach, conducted the secular ceremony. He had become a Reverend to marry another couple previous to us, and as a dear friend it was just right for him to officiate. Everything went well, more than well. It was an ideal day.

And we needed it. I needed it. Since our arrival in Wisconsin at the end of 2010 after our Austin plans falling apart, things had fallen into place fairly well. But people had started falling out. Two guys I had recently made friends with in Eau Claire died suddenly. One went in a car accident, the other by his own hand and a bullet. A long time family friend who I called "Aunt" passed. An older cousin who was also very close to my Mom left her devastated and feeling more alone than ever. My friends Ed and Terry from The Chicago Actors Studio were a great couple, beautifully in love. The last time I spoke with Terry, her cancer was back. She asked me how it was going with Megan. I told her what I told Ed; I found my Terry. I received a phone call from one of the studio interns while on break between students. Terry had passed. Another phone call came from St. Petersburg, Florida. Megan and I had been down there in 2010 for some shows. While there, we hung out with my old music buddy from Chicago. Everyone called him Hollywood. His name was Phil. His wife called me one afternoon. He had died of a massive heart attack, and he was younger than I. His last words were, "Don't forget to put the clothes in the dryer." At least one of them snuck a chuckle from me at the end.

So, our wedding was a nice break from all the losses. It truly was a celebration of life and our two lives together. It was poignant for me. I had not too long before given up on love. Now I was marrying someone who really was an amazing partner in life. We skipped many of the traditional wedding things like the father-daughter dance, and outlawed anything involved "The Chicken Dance," "YMCA," or any other group assimilating sorts of things. I did throw the garter. She did throw the bouquet. I sang "Sea of Love" to her from a wireless microphone as we danced. We cried through our vows. So did everybody else, including The Reverend Teach.

My Mom, Lilias Circle, was no longer mobile and

suffering from some dementia. She generally knew what was going on, but could hardly speak, except with her eyes. A very thoughtful friend of mine called the home where my Mom was and had the nurses put our wedding ceremony on speaker phone while it broadcast live from the site. Two days later, Megan and I visited my Mom at the retirement home. While we spoke with her about the wedding and life in Wisconsin, I wheeled her around in her chair, and she grinned, her eyes alighted with delight. She didn't have to speak for me to know how she felt. And yet she did speak. While I went to her room to check on things and see that the home was looking after my Dear Ole Ma appropriately, she held Megan's hand and very slowly and deliberately said,

"Oh, my, it's wonderful. I am so happy for you both."

I missed it. When we left, I kissed my Mom and told her I loved her. Her lips moved in an effort. Her eyes looked sweet, but sad. Megan and I went back to the hotel, and a few days later we were back at work in Eau Claire.

On August 28, 2011, two weeks to the day after Megan and I joined hands in marriage, my mother, Lilias Circle, passed away in her sleep.

How Phil Got More Hip

At my wedding I was using a cane much of the time. My hip had been giving me serious trouble for a while, and I still hadn't received an accurate diagnosis. After about a year of searching and tolerating extreme pain, I finally got an answer. I had osteonecrosis. The bones in my hip were dying. It's a vascular thing brought on when blood flow to the bones stops. My right hip was in pieces, and I was trying to walk on it. I heavily medicated myself through the pain with booze. I preferred that to pills. I never found pills very social. Booze happened to be part of why my hip died. Heavy drinking combined with extensive use of corticosteroids for asthma and leaping about on stage for 25 years had created the perfect hip storm.

After putting off the impending surgery at the insistence of the doctor who had diagnosed it... I was pretty young, you can only do the surgery a couple times in your life, and you will need to... I finally called him and said I couldn't take it anymore. We scheduled my surgery.

On June 25, 2012, I had what turned out to be one of the fastest complete hip replacement surgeries in the history of surgeries by Dr. Leland Mayer at Mayo Clinic. As he described it to me, backed up by an acquaintance of mine who actually handed him the titanium hip, he cut open my ass cheek and more or less poured out the fragments that remained of my ball joint. From there, there was a little sawing, some precise drilling, two screws, some hammering, and they stapled it shut. I had a new titanium hip and a way to get through airports quicker. I was now more hip than ever and Mayo ended up covering the entire surgery, all $65,000 of it. I recovered fairly quickly. A couple weeks later, I was able to ride with Megan down to Chicago with crutches and guitar in hand. The guys in Chicago were doing a memorial concert for a musician friend we'd lost the prior year…

The Last And Lasting Days Of Matteo

In December of 2011, I received a phone call from my friend and brother in music of 20 years, groomsman at my wedding to Megan, and the man that taught me plenty about the blues, the biz, and live performance. I had last seen him on a trip back to Chicago for my Mom's memorial in October where he and I and our wives sat together on his front stoop and spoke at great length. He was finishing his last round of chemo for his second valiant fight with cancer. He seemed confident it was working and that he'd win the battle again. I wasn't so sure. Two weeks before my Mom's passing, Matt stood at my wedding, escorted a bridesmaid down the aisle, looking emaciated. He had told me that he would be there even if he was puking on the side of the road from his treatments.

"There's no way I'm missing this, hermano," he said.

This was from the man who had attended my previous two weddings and was one of the few who had good reason to understand the importance of this one.

"Felipe, you finally got it right, my brother."

Then one day in December, just before Christmas, I received a voice message on my cellphone, one I prayed my intuition was wrong about:

"Hey Felipe, it's Matteo. I dunno, get in touch with me soon if you can. Make a long story short, I'm in hospice now as you know. Time's running really short for me. Really, really short, man. So short, I don't think you'll be able to make it down here in time. I love you my brother, I don't really know how to say goodbye, never been good at that sorta thing, but I guess I have to. I just dunno what the fuck to say, but please try and get in touch with me if you can and we'll rap a bit. I love you my Felipe, my brother."

I went outside the music school in Eau Claire, where I was teaching private lessons. I lit a smoke, braced myself, and called him back. We got to speak for a good amount of time. I promised him Megan and I and all he considered La Familia would look after his wife Barbie, and would always honor his music. He reflected on what a great ride he'd had. I thanked him for being true family. We even laughed a little. He said,

"You know I'm glad, my brother, that you don't sound sad, that you're being upbeat. You have to know that I'm at peace with my God and I'll look in on you on occasion. If you hear a little harp (harmonica) in the wind, it'll be me. You give Megan my love, will ya? She's a doll. Again, you finally got it right."

When we were done talking and said our final goodbyes, I hung up the phone, leaned against the wall of the school, and wept convulsively. There was no way I was going to let him know I was in so much pain, because he brought so much pleasure to so many. It seemed only right that he still know that was the case, right up until the end. I wanted his last thoughts of our brotherhood to be good ones, not worrisome ones. The song I wrote "Just the Blues Ma'am" says,

"I speak to him nightly and he speaks to me back."

It's true. I have little conversations with him in my mind's ear and in my dreams. We talk about life and music, just as if he's right next to me having a smoke and a beer. I look to the sky and ask him with a smile, "What do ya think, Matteo?" when something goes well. I hear him laugh. For all I know he is. This man's legacy lives through the myriad friends, family, fans, and other musicians that he influenced. The remarkable work he did, and his general approach to life, was encompassed in this maxim... live it well, then be at peace.

Lem Roby and I are at Matteo's Memorial, along with a long list of fellow Chicago musicians. He and I have been asked to play "Blackbird" by The Beatles (we all know it's a McCartney tune). Barb, Matt's widow, had explained that it was one of his favorite songs. I was a little surprised. I hadn't known. He was always the subtle philosopher and would leave some things vague enough for you to have to find it of your own accord.

Neither Lem nor I think we can emotionally deal with it, despite 20 years of playing music together, or perhaps *as a result* of having also played so much of the music with Matthew "Matteo" Steinmetz.

I'm always an emotional wreck in these circumstances. Lem normally handles similar situations with humor and a seriously brilliant and insightful wisdom. Ask him, I call him often while I'm in some breakdown, and he resets my perspective like he's restarting a computer. Today, it takes all either or both of us have to not completely fall apart at the loss of our dear friend.

Lem plays the guitar part while I sing the lyrics. We stare at each other to avoid the tears of those around us and for fear of crumbling and not honoring our friend as we intend. We meditate on our joined musical life with this man, for the strength of it. With looks in our eyes of loss, then love, and finally pride, we somehow get through. We knew this man, he loved us, we loved him. We all shared it and it remains.

Matteo's Eulogy was given by another mutual musical brother and friend of many of those present, whom we all affectionately called Dougie. He joined Matteo two years later.

When you work so emotionally close with someone, creating at such remarkable levels, even using your occasional creative and personal differences as fodder for the cannon and fuel for the fire... you become, even if you try not to be... irrevocably connected. You never get over it, you simply keep alive the beauty of what you have lived.

And Then He Got Sober

There Goes His Reputation

You know the story.

Here's the set up:

It had become well known to my fans that I enjoyed it when they'd bring shots to the stage and place them at my feet. I'd grab them and knock 'em back while playing guitar one-handed or turn away while a band mate would snatch one up while I acted as if I wasn't watching, or make some other move of mock showmanship. It was a (deadly) bonding experience between my audience and me. This night was no different.

Here's the pitch:

I'm on stage at Chicago's Double Door on a Saturday night before a standing-room-only crowd. I look down. There are seven shots of tequila. I shrug my shoulders and reach for one. Then another. People cheer. And the next. They egg me on. Soon, all of the shots have made their way into my addicted body and I think I'm feeling the warm fuzzies.

And the swing:

The emcee grabs the microphone and gives a brief and flattering run down of who I am and ends with, "Ladies and gentleman, Phil Circle!"

And the strike (or was it a hit?), as I strut to the mic amongst applause and let go in a grandiose way with,

"Go fuck yourself! A one, two, three… "

And the band and I kick into our set.

But this wasn't the worst of it. Neither was my 10-minute version of a song that usually goes six; or my raunchy comments during the show; or that my drummer quit after this last straw. The worst part of this evening was the response I received. People loved it. They wanted to see me abuse myself and share my pain with them. They wanted the spectacle. When I left the stage I was patted on the back and "treated" to more free drinks. The other bands of the evening all complimented my show. The manager of one of the bands asked me why such a professional group as mine was even sharing a stage with the other bands. I was encouraged to act this way! I was given a free pass to be an ass! I was told in no uncertain terms (that is, I heard it this way) that it's perfectly fine if I rage in my alcoholism and let it affect my gift... the music.

I don't know if this was the beginning of the end for me and I just didn't see it. I don't know if this was the arc of my disease taking over. I don't know if I realized yet the damage I was doing to myself physically, mentally, and spiritually. Most drunks and druggies can't find that key point in the progress of their illness. But I do know this. From that show right up until I had enough, I used that evening as one of many examples of how great I was. How sick is that? Loaded question.

When I look back at my 30-plus years of playing music, I see a trend. Every time I got a pat on my back, it went to my head. I guess there's an "activate ego" button on my upper vertebrae. Once it went to my head, I felt as if I didn't need to give as much or work as hard. Oh, but I could still drink as hard. When that led to fewer gigs and smaller crowds, I blamed the music business and the public's poor ear for talent. When this led to resentments, I drank even more. All of this would restart several times until the pats on the back became fewer and turned into skewed glances of concern or scrunched-up wincing faces. I reached the bottom.

It wasn't the pancreatitis with its excruciating pain and puking blood that made me quit drinking. It wasn't the liver disease. It wasn't the loss of my livelihood. It wasn't the many ways I was wasting away physically or the potential loss of my best friend, my wife. It wasn't that my spirit had been squashed and replaced with a debilitating painful despair. The final straw was the difficult realization and admission that I no longer had my art. The thing I loved the most in the world; the means by which I shared my genuine love for people; the gift the universe gave me; it was gone.

When I went to treatment, the first thing my very insightful substance abuse counselor did was put me with a spiritual counselor who was also a guitarist to discuss grieving. What was I grieving, I asked. The loss of your music, he answered. Shortly, my treatment plan had among the various readings and exercises of humility an assignment that scared the crap out of me. I was to play a set of music… just me, my voice, and my guitar… for the 25 guys in my unit. Sober. No meds. I had only coffee and Skittles to get me by, and the loving encouragement of a bunch of guys who were strangers to me a couple weeks prior. From that first of several performances to my fellow inmates in treatment, my music came back.

When I returned home to Wisconsin, I was asked to play an opening solo set for a woman whose band I had blacked out in front of at my last show just before leaving for the sober woods up north. She introduced me by telling the story of my previous show, dirt and all. She ended her story by saying that now she sees a different man in Phil Circle. Instead of a cocky strutting rooster, she sees a humble and loving man who just wants to share his gift of music.

"Shit," I thought, "that's all I ever wanted to do."

Afterwards, she posted online that I "absolutely kicked ass." I got teary and felt a strangely different reaction. I wanted to work hard to keep giving something, not taking. I knew this was going to require a lot of hard work, both physically and at a spiritual level. I keep busy in Buddhism. I keep busy with my guitar and voice. I keep writing. I'm thrilled if three people enjoy something I share. Suddenly, I remember why I started doing this. I love to give. I don't really care for the so-called rock star image. I don't want it. I never did. I became immersed in the throes of a disease that pushed for any excuse to stay alive, even at the expense of my life. And a funny thing has happened at shows. No one asks me if I want a drink. They just tell me how glad they are I quit. And that button on my back when you pat it? It's turned into an "activate gratitude" button.

The Finals

Wrap It Up, I'll Take It

Well, there it is. That's where I stand today. My story isn't through, and I look forward to more. I don't have some profound message. I didn't finally crawl from some muddy swamp to blossom like a lotus flower or something. I've just survived. Somewhere between my self-pity and arrogance, I've found a middle ground, a humble confidence. I balance there, sometimes teetering, sometimes walking with an element of grace. I've made my bed and I haven't. I've made all kinds of choices that simply land in one of two columns: skilled or unskilled. Luck has helped. Resilience has, too. A photographer I worked with used the word *grit*. I'll take it. But it's a sort of fine grit. It's like the volcanic dust of fires born to create a new landscape, a new world on which to walk. And when I wash it off, that nine-year-old kid dancing down LaSalle Street emerges with his dreams of music. I'm not sure what kind of kid he was. One brother of mine said I was a sweet kid. One of my sisters said I was a little shit. They're probably both right.

Should life be easy or hard? Should we try to change things or go with the flow? Should we live with who we are or make moves to improve our perceptions? Are there mores to follow or have we simply created them for assimilation of the masses? Are we geniuses or fools? I answer all of these questions emphatically "Yes." I am of one firm conviction: I have lived my life to this point as I and it saw fit, in order for me to be the man I am today. Whatever the causes made, I'll suffer the effects or rejoice in them. Teetering or walking gracefully, I will continue to move forward. I will continue to survive and at times thrive beautifully. One thing is damned certain: I'm still here for some reason. I'll keep looking for it in the arts.

I hope you've found something worth your time in these pages. I hope you find something worthwhile in yourself and your work. Thanks for reading.

Hold your head up.

Peace, love, and the arts,

-Phil Circle

I was born at Evanston Hospital, Illinois, on April 12, 1966, to Lilias Wagner Jones and Robert Leslie Jones. I was given the names Phillip (handed down from Phillip Wagner born in 1847) and Thomas (after Thomas a Kempis the writer). When I was eight months old, my parents divorced and at age two, my mother married Thomas Robert (Bob) Circle, who eventually adopted me, giving him the name Circle.

Lilias Wagner (now) Circle was a musician and writer with a Masters in English. She played viola and piano and sang alto. As a producer of Gilbert and Sullivan Operettas, she became the first woman ever to produce all fourteen G&S operettas in the U.S.

Bob Circle was an economist from The University of Chicago, all-but-dissertation, and a great raconteur who inspired me to tell stories with flair. He carried this tradition from his father Earl Circle, his Uncles Dave, Rhys, Charno and Tom Jones, and especially his older cousin, Steve Richards. Steve brought my Dad to Chicago when he was 10 years old for the 1933 World's Fair. Steve was a reporter and wrote a book called The Biggest Sycamore. It's about the little part of Appalachia where they grew up. I've read it. It's a short and very fun read. In it are stories my Dad used to tell at dinner.

My biological father, Bob Jones, studied physics at Harvard until he got a B and his father, a lawyer and politician, Leslie Jones told him he was going into law "like all the Joneses before him." He got his law degree at

213

University of Michigan where he met my Mom. His mother Agnes Woodward Jones had graduated from The Art Institute of Chicago at the time of Georgia O'Kieffe, but Les wouldn't allow her to pursue the arts. I knew my Grandparents Jones, but didn't meet my father until I lived in New Mexico. We got along surprisingly well and kept a healthy relationship until he passed in 2015.

My Dad Circle was also previously married to Barbara Fisher. By his description, she was a very impressive woman. They rode their tandem bicycle across The Alps for their honeymoon. She passed in 1966 from cancer. Barb and Circ had two kids, my brother Tom Circle, and my sister Jane Circle-Asmuth.

Tom owns a pool and spa company, and can dismantle and rebuild a car with his eyes closed. Jane is a PhD in electrical engineering who can dismantle and rebuild the universe in a short paragraph. On the Jones side, I have a younger half brother from Jones' second marriage. His name is Gunther. I've met him all of about six times and like him a lot. My immediate blood includes three more elder siblings. Eric Jones is the next youngest after me, and carries an MBA but prefers to dismantle and beautifully rebuild homes. Bob is a PhD in psychology who enjoys dismantling the human mind and rebuilding the industrial-organizational world through teaching and being quoted in Forbes. Bob is also the other musician in the family. We've played shows together twice. Our matron is my oldest sibling and sister, Lilias Jones-Jarding. She carries a PhD in political science and is very effective at dismantling the bullshit. She is gradually rebuilding the world through her work as a political activist and professor. She has more tattoos than me, doesn't drink or smoke, and drives a Harley-Davidson. She likes chocolate.

I admire and love my family very much and this little brother dedicates this book to their guidance and love as we move into becoming the elder generation with an aim to dismantle and rebuild the world left to us. But there is one more to whom I dedicate this book...

She floated past me like Lauren Bacall...

...I was reclining in a corner seat at the actors' studio. I had been over at The Bucktown Pub having afternoon drinks with the guys from Harpo Studios when I received a call from one of the interns. He told me she was coming by for her interview. I swallowed my beer and came back to the studio to participate in a little stargazing. She moved past me with the grace of someone who knew her strength or at the very least pretended to. I followed with an air of cool and took a seat across from her in the office. While the intern questioned her, I pretended to work on the other computer while trying to subtly size her up. She looked in her early twenties, but spoke and acted in her early thirties. It turned out she was the former. I could just glance her long carved face framed by her long straightened hair, her supple lips letting loose an advanced vocabulary in the sultry voice of a starlet. I assessed her overall shape and found I approved wholeheartedly.

I slyly tested her by making a clever remark at the intern's expense. She retorted with equal or greater cleverness. I made an obscure reference and she got it. "This one's good," I thought. She's more than good. I began my plans to get to know her a little better at complete risk to the brick walls of my destitute heart. I knew the dangers. I could see them right in front of me. My inner voice said, "Don't do it, man. You know these women are all out to get you!" I told it to fuck off and went in anyway. It took me five indirect and frail attempts, but she finally let me take her out. She told me she might as well get it over with.

When I found out that we both were fans of Bogey and Bacall, Lord Of The Rings, and Monty Python, I knew it was meant to be. "I'm gonna marry this girl," I told myself. I did.

Thanks sweetheart for joining me on this incredible ride without brakes. Your saintly patience, tremendous courage, beautiful laughing smile and overall brilliance have been a source of strength and support. Your love has been an inspiration. I lubber you babr!

If you try to restrain the fire within you,
It will burn you up from the inside out,
If you let it flare and fuel its flames,
It will lift you up without a doubt.

-Phil Circle, 1986, written from a hospital bed.